HOUSE of WHITE BIRCHES

75

Merry Christmas

PROJECTS
in Plastic
Canvas

Edited by
Laura
Scott

HOUSE of
WHITE
BIRCHES

PUBLISHERS
SINCE 1947

75 Merry Christmas Projects in Plastic Canvas

Copyright © 1999 House of White Birches, Berne, Indiana 46711

Editor: Laura Scott
Associate Editor: June Sprunger
Copy Editor: Mary Nowak
Publications Coordinator: Myra Moore
Design Coordinator: Tanya Turner
Technical Artists: Pam Gregory, Allison Rothe, Jessica Rothe

Photographers: Tammy Christian, Jeff Chilcote, Jennifer Foreman
Photography Stylist: Arlou Wittwer
Photography Assistant: Linda Quinlan

Production Supervisor/Artist: Ronda Bollenbacher
Production Coordinator: Brenda Gallmeyer
Creative Coordinator: Shaun Venish
Book Design: Klaus Rothe
Cover Design: Dan Kraner
Traffic Coordinator: Sandra Beres
Production Assistants: Shirley Blalock, Dana Brotherton, Carol Dailey

Publishers: Carl H. Muselman, Arthur K. Muselman
Chief Executive Officer: John Robinson
Marketing Director: Scott Moss
Editorial Director: Vivian Rothe
Production Director: George Hague

Printed in the United States of America
First Printing: 1999
Library of Congress Number: 99-94089
ISBN: 1-882138-46-5

Ayriel Lortie from Charmaine Model Agency, Fort Wayne, Ind., modeled for chapter one.

Front cover projects, clockwise from top left: Poinsettia Gift Bag, page 125; Snow Angel, page 12; Rocking Rudy, page 151; Very Merry Ornaments, page 8; Snowball Stand Tissue Topper, page 115. Back cover projects, clockwise from top left: Keepsake Christmas Frame, page 54; Christmas Tree Gift Bag, page 122; Mr. Snowman's Bath, page 107; Holiday Lighthouse, page 154; Snowbirdie Box, page 132.

Holiday Greetings!

Christmas has been a favorite holiday for bringing families together for centuries. Most of us spend the last few months of each year preparing for holiday dinners and the opening of presents on Christmas morning. Decorating for the season and exchanging special hand-crafted gifts are among the most creative of traditions.

For this terrific volume of Merry Christmas projects, our best plastic canvas designers have created an exciting range of Christmas designs to add sparkle and fun to your holiday decorating and gift-giving.

Our chapters include your favorite themes-extra-special ornaments and trims, thoughtful gifts to stitch in a jiffy, welcome-home country accents, playful teddy bears, jolly snowmen and much more. We were careful to keep the materials and supplies for these great designs simple and straightforward so you can enjoy relatively stress-free shopping at your nearby craft store.

Many of these projects are simple enough for children to work on. You may want to begin a Christmas tradition of having each child or grandchild choose a project, then start stitching it with you on Christmas day. This is a wonderful way to spend time with your youngsters, introducing them to a hobby that they may come to enjoy as much as you do.

As you work through your favorite projects just before the holiday season and throughout the year, may your mind be filled with happy thoughts of friends and family, Christmases past and Christmases to come.

Wishing you many happy holidays,

Laura Scott

Editor
75 Merry Christmas Projects in Plastic Canvas

Table of Contents

Home for Christmas

Christmas Wrappings

A White Christmas

Extras

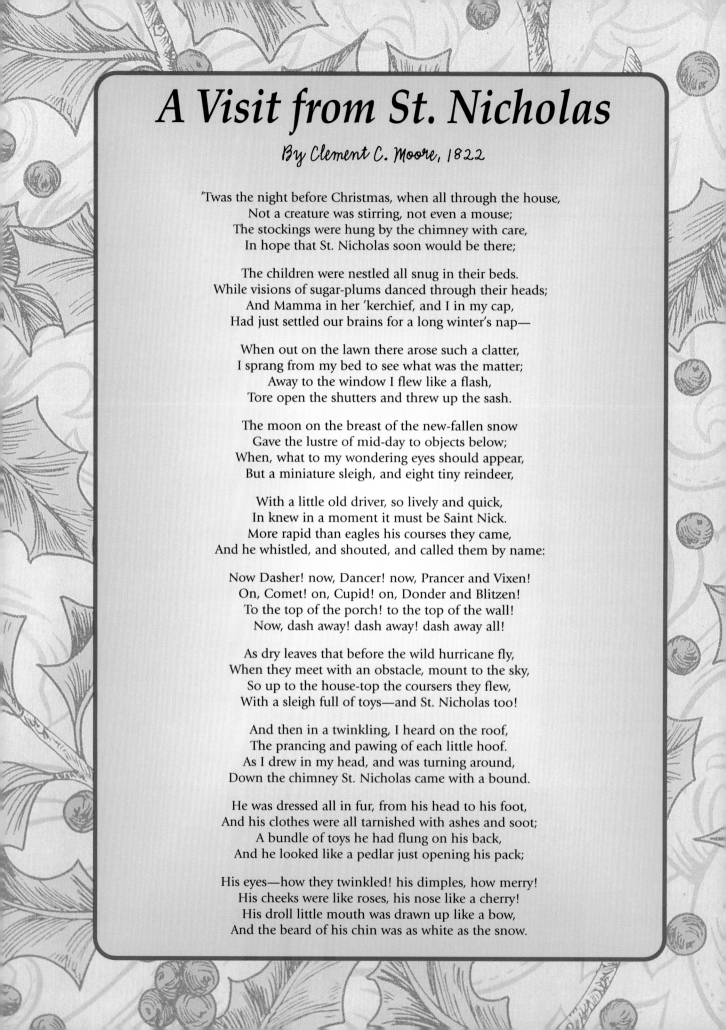

A Visit from St. Nicholas

By Clement C. Moore, 1822

'Twas the night before Christmas, when all through the house,
Not a creature was stirring, not even a mouse;
The stockings were hung by the chimney with care,
In hope that St. Nicholas soon would be there;

The children were nestled all snug in their beds.
While visions of sugar-plums danced through their heads;
And Mamma in her 'kerchief, and I in my cap,
Had just settled our brains for a long winter's nap—

When out on the lawn there arose such a clatter,
I sprang from my bed to see what was the matter;
Away to the window I flew like a flash,
Tore open the shutters and threw up the sash.

The moon on the breast of the new-fallen snow
Gave the lustre of mid-day to objects below;
When, what to my wondering eyes should appear,
But a miniature sleigh, and eight tiny reindeer,

With a little old driver, so lively and quick,
In knew in a moment it must be Saint Nick.
More rapid than eagles his courses they came,
And he whistled, and shouted, and called them by name:

Now Dasher! now, Dancer! now, Prancer and Vixen!
On, Comet! on, Cupid! on, Donder and Blitzen!
To the top of the porch! to the top of the wall!
Now, dash away! dash away! dash away all!

As dry leaves that before the wild hurricane fly,
When they meet with an obstacle, mount to the sky,
So up to the house-top the coursers they flew,
With a sleigh full of toys—and St. Nicholas too!

And then in a twinkling, I heard on the roof,
The prancing and pawing of each little hoof.
As I drew in my head, and was turning around,
Down the chimney St. Nicholas came with a bound.

He was dressed all in fur, from his head to his foot,
And his clothes were all tarnished with ashes and soot;
A bundle of toys he had flung on his back,
And he looked like a pedlar just opening his pack;

His eyes—how they twinkled! his dimples, how merry!
His cheeks were like roses, his nose like a cherry!
His droll little mouth was drawn up like a bow,
And the beard of his chin was as white as the snow.

A Festival of Trees

Create a tradition by stitching a collection of festive and vibrant ornaments your family will look forward to hanging year after year!

SLEIGH RIDES 5¢

Stitch and share this delightful trio

A Festival of Trees

Beginner
Skill Level

Stitch this threesome of cheery ornaments to add a bright and colorful touch to your tree. A huggable gingerbread man, country plaid bow and heart-shaped basket are a delight to stitch and share!

Materials

Hearts & Holly Basket

□ ½ sheet Uniek Quick-Count 7-count plastic canvas

□ Uniek Needloft plastic canvas yarn as listed in color key

□ #16 tapestry needle

□ 13 (4mm) ruby Austrian glass rhinestones #110-636-09 from National Artcraft

□ Crafter's Pick Jewel Bond glue from Adhesive Products Inc.

□ Hot-glue gun

Continued on page 10

Hearts & Holly Basket

Instructions

1 Cut plastic canvas according to graphs (page 10).

2 Stitch pieces following graphs. Work Backstitches on handle and Straight Stitches on holly leaves when background stitching is completed.

3 Overcast handle, holly leaves, white heart and small heart with adjacent colors.

4 Using red throughout, Overcast top edges on basket front and back from dot to dot. Overcast one short end on each basket side; Whip-stitch remaining short ends together. Whipstitch sides to front and back.

5 Using photo as a guide and hot glue throughout, center and glue white heart to basket front. Glue three holly leaves to center of white heart, then glue small heart to center of holly leaf cluster. Glue handle to basket sides.

6 With jewel glue, attach rhinestones to handle and holly leaves where indicated on graphs.

Gingerbread Man Surprise

Instructions

1 Cut plastic canvas according to graphs (page 11).

2 Stitch pieces following graphs. Work Christmas red pearl cotton Backstitches on top front when background stitching is completed.

3 With sewing needle and black thread, sew heart beads to top front and bottom front where indicated on graphs. Using photo as a guide, glue cabochons for eyes to top front.

4 Using maple through step 5, Overcast bottom edge of top

front and top edge of bottom front.

5 Matching edges and with wrong sides facing, Whipstitch top front to back around arms and head from blue dot to blue dot, then Whipstitch bottom front to back around sides and bottom, working through all three layers at waistline where top and bottom overlap.

6 Attach 8" length green pearl cotton to center top of head with a Lark's Head Knot (Fig. 1). Tie ends in a knot to form a loop for hanging.

Fig. 1
Lark's Head Knot

7 Cut two 3" lengths of rickrack. Using photo for placement, wrap one length around bottom of each leg and glue in place on backside. Repeat with remaining 2" length of rickrack, wrapping around arm on left.

8 With matching thread, sew candy cane button to hand on right. Tie plaid ribbon in a bow; trim ends. Glue bow to top front between mouth and top heart button.

9 Tuck money, greeting, candy cane or small gift into front pocket.

Country Plaid Bow

Instructions

1 Cut plastic canvas according to graphs (page 11).

2 Stitch pieces following graphs, reversing one tail before stitching. Work gold Backstitches using 6 strands floss when background stitching is completed. Overcast following graphs.

Very Merry Ornaments

Continued from page 9

Materials

Gingerbread Man Surprise

- ☐ ½ sheet Uniek Quick-Count 7-count plastic canvas
- ☐ Uniek Needloft plastic canvas yarn as listed in color key
- ☐ 8" green DMC #3 pearl cotton and as listed in color key
- ☐ #16 tapestry needle
- ☐ 8" green baby rickrack
- ☐ 12" 1½"-wide red plaid ribbon
- ☐ 5 (8mm) red glass heart beads #5-128 from Creative Beginnings
- ☐ 2 (6mm) round black cabochons from The Beadery
- ☐ Candy cane button
- ☐ Sewing needle
- ☐ Black sewing thread
- ☐ Sewing thread to match candy cane button
- ☐ Hot-glue gun

Country Plaid Bow

- ☐ ½ sheet Uniek Quick-Count 7-count plastic canvas
- ☐ Uniek Needloft plastic canvas yarn as listed in color key
- ☐ DMC 6-strand metallic embroidery floss as listed in color key
- ☐ #16 tapestry needle
- ☐ 9" x 12" sheet white felt
- ☐ 10.5mm x 10mm ruby heart cabochon from The Beadery
- ☐ Hot-glue gun

3 Using bow and tails as templates, cut felt slightly smaller than each piece; glue to backsides.

4 Using photo as a guide, glue tails to back of bow. Center and glue knot to bow front. Glue three holly leaves to bow front, directly under knot, then glue heart cabochon to center of holly leaf cluster.

5 For hanger, cut a 36" length of embroidery floss. Tie ends together in a knot, forming a large circle. Loop circle over index fingers of both hands. Twist fingers in opposite directions, twisting cord until it begins to loop back on itself. Place both loops on one index finger, folding floss in half; allow halves to twist around each other.

6 Insert ends of twisted floss from front to back through holes on bow where indicated on graph. Tie ends in a knot on backside. ●

COLOR KEY
HEARTS & HOLLY BASKET

Plastic Canvas Yarn	Yards
■ Christmas red #02	14
■ Holly #27	7
☐ White #41	3
╱ Holly #27 Backstitch and Straight Stitch	
● Attach ruby rhinestone	

Color numbers given are for Uniek Needloft plastic canvas yarn.

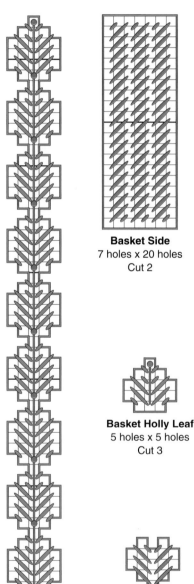

Basket Side
7 holes x 20 holes
Cut 2

Basket Holly Leaf
5 holes x 5 holes
Cut 3

Basket Handle
5 holes x 54 holes
Cut 1

Small Heart
5 holes x 5 holes
Cut 1

Basket Front & Back
19 holes x 19 holes
Cut 2

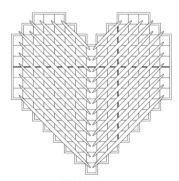

White Heart
15 holes x 15 holes
Cut 1

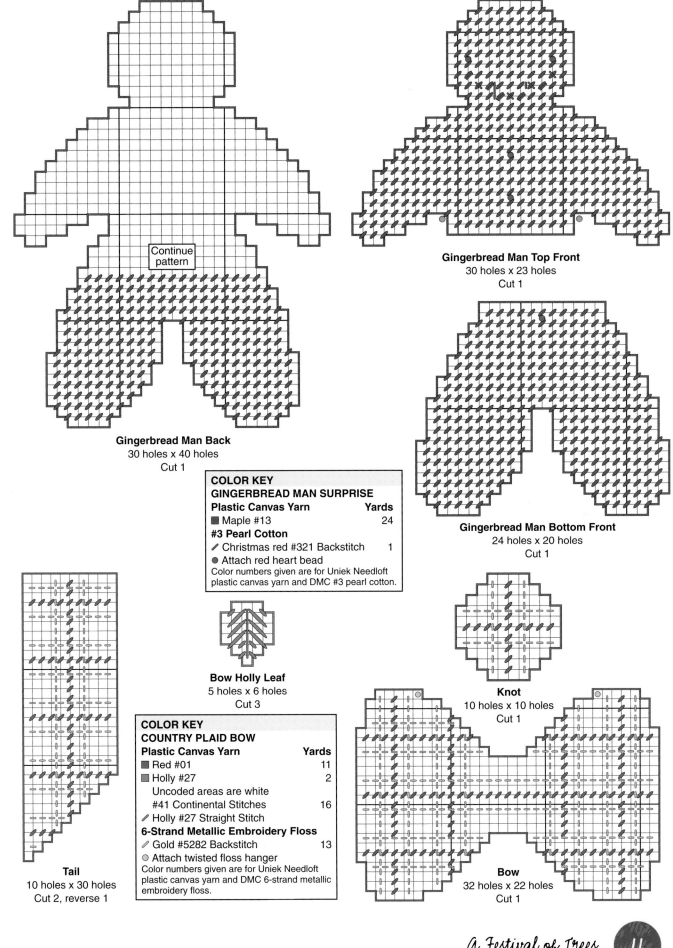

Gingerbread Man Back
30 holes x 40 holes
Cut 1

Continue pattern

Gingerbread Man Top Front
30 holes x 23 holes
Cut 1

Gingerbread Man Bottom Front
24 holes x 20 holes
Cut 1

COLOR KEY
GINGERBREAD MAN SURPRISE

Plastic Canvas Yarn	Yards
■ Maple #13	24

#3 Pearl Cotton

✎ Christmas red #321 Backstitch	1
● Attach red heart bead	

Color numbers given are for Uniek Needloft plastic canvas yarn and DMC #3 pearl cotton.

Bow Holly Leaf
5 holes x 6 holes
Cut 3

Knot
10 holes x 10 holes
Cut 1

COLOR KEY
COUNTRY PLAID BOW

Plastic Canvas Yarn	Yards
■ Red #01	11
■ Holly #27	2
Uncoded areas are white #41 Continental Stitches	16
✎ Holly #27 Straight Stitch	

6-Strand Metallic Embroidery Floss

✎ Gold #5282 Backstitch	13
● Attach twisted floss hanger	

Color numbers given are for Uniek Needloft plastic canvas yarn and DMC 6-strand metallic embroidery floss.

Tail
10 holes x 30 holes
Cut 2, reverse 1

Bow
32 holes x 22 holes
Cut 1

Snow Angel

Design by Vicki Blizzard

Stitch a little hint of heavenly grace

Cutting & Stitching

1 Cut plastic canvas according to graphs (page 13), cutting away gray areas on halo and head pieces.

2 Stitch pieces following graphs, reversing one hand before stitching. Overcast scepter following graphs, then work gold Straight Stitch on scepter handle.

3 Overcast halo heart, cheeks and hands with adjacent colors. Overcast inside and outside edges of halo with gold.

4 With white pearl, Whipstitch wrong sides of two wings together. Repeat with remaining two wings.

5 With sewing needle and white thread, sew buttons to body front and bead to center of head front for nose as in photo.

6 Using white throughout, Whipstitch wrong sides of body front and back together.

7 Overcast bottom edge of both head front and back from blue dot to blue dot. With wrong sides facing, Whipstitch remaining edges of head front and back together.

Assembly

1 Using photo as a guide through step 5 and using hot glue through step 2, insert body into bottom opening of head; glue in place. Glue cheeks to face, wings to back of body, and halo to back of head.

A Festival of Trees

Intermediate
Skill Level

Add a heavenly touch to your tree with this delightful snow angel ornament!

Materials

- □ ½ sheet Uniek Quick-Count 7-count plastic canvas
- □ 5 (3") plastic canvas radial circles by Darice
- □ Uniek Needloft plastic canvas yarn as listed in color key
- □ ⅛"-wide Plastic Canvas 7 Metallic Needlepoint Yarn by Rainbow Gallery as listed in color key
- □ #16 tapestry needle
- □ 2 (7mm) round black cabochons from The Beadery
- □ 5 (5mm) round black cabochons from The Beadery
- □ 6mm ruby round acrylic faceted bead from The Beadery
- □ 3 (⅜") red buttons
- □ 8" of ⅜"-wide red pin-dot ribbon from Wrights
- □ Sewing needle and white thread
- □ Crafter's Pick Jewel Bond glue from Adhesive Products Inc.
- □ Hot-glue gun

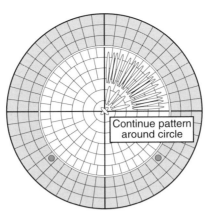

Angel Head Front & Back
Cut 2

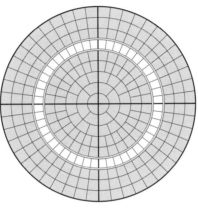

Angel Halo
Cut 1
Do not stitch

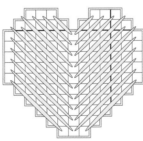

Angel Wing
13 holes x 12 holes
Cut 4

Angel Body Front & Back
Stitch 2

Halo Heart
3 holes x 3 holes
Cut 1

Angel Cheek
3 holes x 3 holes
Cut 2

Angel Hand
7 holes x 6 holes
Cut 2, reverse 1

Scepter
5 holes x 17 holes
Cut 4

COLOR KEY	
Plastic Canvas Yarn	**Yards**
■ Red #02	1
□ Pink #07	1
■ Holly #27	2
□ White #41	13
⅛" Metallic Needlepoint Yarn	
□ White pearl #PC10	8
⟋ Yellow gold #PC7 Straight Stitch and Overcasting	2
Color numbers given are for Uniek Needloft plastic canvas yarn and Rainbow Gallery Plastic Canvas 7 Metallic Needlepoint Yarn.	

2 Glue halo heart to left side of halo. Glue scepter to back of right mitten, then glue mittens to body.

3 With jewel glue, attach 7mm black cabochons to head for eyes and 5mm black cabochons to head for mouth.

4 Tie ribbon in a small bow; trim ends. Hot-glue bow to left side of body just below head.

5 Cut a 12" length of white pearl yarn. Thread ends from front to back through center holes at top of head. Tie ends in a bow to form a loop for hanging. ●

Santa's Helpers

Designs by Celia Lange Designs

Hang these year after year

Reindeer

Instructions

1 Cut and stitch plastic canvas according to graphs (pages 15 and 16), reversing one hoof and one ear before stitching. Work uncoded areas on hooves with brown Continental Stitches.

2 Overcast following graphs. Work Backstitches with black pearl cotton when stitching and Overcasting are completed.

3 For antlers, cut florist wire in half and bend each following Fig. 1. Paint wood on chalkboard holly green; let dry.

**Fig. 1
Antler**

4 Using photo as a guide through step 9, cut a ¾" length of toothpick. With white paint pen, paint toothpick for chalk; print "SLEIGH RIDES 5¢" on chalkboard; let dry.

5 Cut desired length of doll hair and glue to center back of head. then bring hair over forehead. Unravel, trim and glue in place.

6 Fold ribbon in a "V" at center point; secure with a stitch. Stitch small jingle bells to ribbon.

Glue ribbon with bells to front of body; fold ends over shoulders and glue to back.

7 Stitch or glue red button to muzzle for nose. Glue muzzle to lower front part of face; glue ears and antlers to top backside of head. Glue eyes above muzzle. Glue hooves to top front of chalkboard, placing candy cane under one hoof and chalk under remaining hoof. Glue tail to back right side of chalkboard.

8 Glue lower part of body to top backside of chalkboard, then glue brace to back of chalkboard and back of body to stabilize body.

9 Thread gold cord through back brace; tie ends in a knot. Tack cord to back of reindeer to secure.

Elf

Instructions

1 Cut and stitch plastic canvas according to graphs (page 16), reversing one hand and one shoe before stitching.

2 Overcast following graphs. Work Backstitches and Straight Stitches with black pearl cotton when stitching and Overcasting are completed.

3 With green yarn, sew large jingle bell to tip of hat and small jingle bells to tips of shoes.

4 Paint wood on chalkboard Santa red; let dry. Using photo as a guide through step 9, cut a ¾" length of toothpick. With white

Beginner
Skill Level

Stitch this pair of whimsical ornaments for holiday fun and cheer!

Materials

Reindeer

☐ 1 sheet 7-count plastic canvas

☐ Coats & Clark Red Heart Classic worsted weight yarn Art. E267 as listed in color key

☐ DMC #3 pearl cotton as listed in color key

☐ #16 tapestry needle

☐ 18" of 18-gauge green florist wire

☐ 3" x 5" wood-framed chalkboard

☐ DecoArt Americana holly green #DA48 acrylic paint

☐ Paintbrush

☐ Round toothpick

☐ White fine-point paint pen

☐ Small amount blond medium Stringlets 100 percent cotton doll hair by All Cooped Up

☐ Small amount of ¼"-wide red satin ribbon

☐ 3 (6mm) gold jingle bells

☐ Sewing needle and red sewing thread

Continued on page 16

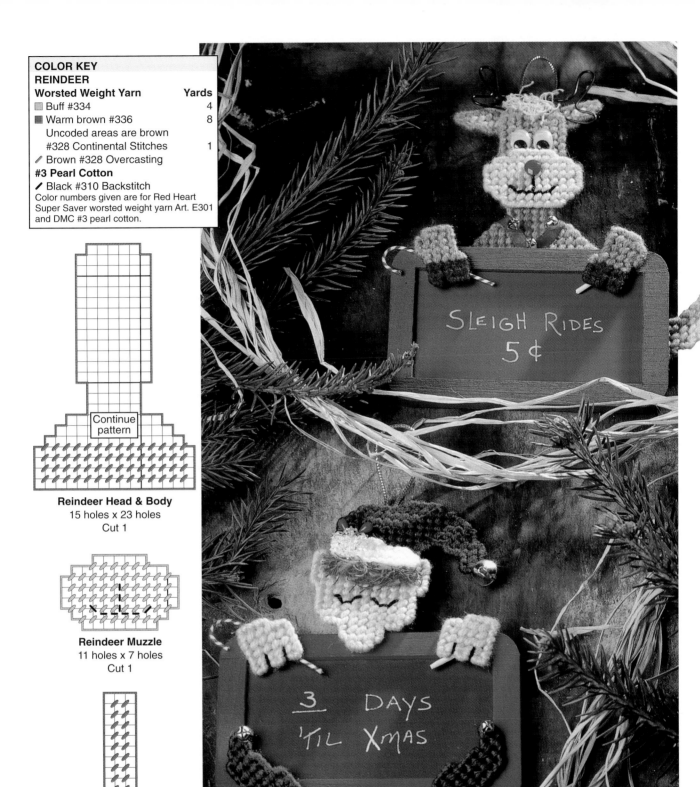

Worsted Weight Yarn	Yards
⬜ Buff #334	4
⬛ Warm brown #336	8
Uncoded areas are brown	
#328 Continental Stitches	1
✎ Brown #328 Overcasting	

#3 Pearl Cotton
✎ Black #310 Backstitch
Color numbers given are for Red Heart Super Saver worsted weight yarn Art. E301 and DMC #3 pearl cotton.

Reindeer Head & Body
15 holes x 23 holes
Cut 1

Continue pattern

Reindeer Muzzle
11 holes x 7 holes
Cut 1

Reindeer Brace
3 holes x 10 holes
Cut 1

paint pen, paint toothpick for chalk; print "3 DAYS 'TIL XMAS" on chalkboard; let dry.

5 Cut desired length of doll hair and glue to back of hat brim, allowing small amount to hang below bottom edge. Unravel and trim as necessary.

6 Glue hat brim to forehead and hat. Glue iridescent snowflake to left side of hat brim and berries to hat above snowflake.

7 Glue shoes to bottom front of chalkboard. Glue hands to top front of chalkboard, placing candy

Materials

Continued from page 14

- ☐ 2 (12mm) oval movable eyes
- ☐ ¼" red shank button
- ☐ 2" miniature thin candy cane
- ☐ 12" gold cord
- ☐ Hot-glue gun

Elf

- ☐ 1 sheet 7-count plastic canvas
- ☐ Coats & Clark Red Heart Classic worsted weight yarn Art. E267 as listed in color key
- ☐ Coats & Clark Red Heart Jeweltones worsted weight yarn Art. E278 as listed in color key
- ☐ DMC #3 pearl cotton as listed in color key
- ☐ #16 tapestry needle
- ☐ 2 (6mm) gold jingle bells
- ☐ 10mm gold jingle bell
- ☐ 3" x 5" wood-framed chalkboard
- ☐ DecoArt Americana Santa red #DA170 acrylic paint
- ☐ Paintbrush
- ☐ Toothpick
- ☐ White fine-point paint pen
- ☐ Small amount auburn medium Stringlets 100 percent cotton doll hair by All Cooped Up
- ☐ ¾" iridescent snowflake
- ☐ 2 small red berries
- ☐ 2" miniature thin candy cane
- ☐ 12" gold cord
- ☐ Hot-glue gun

cane under one hand and chalk under remaining hand.

8 Glue head to center top front of chalkboard so nose hangs over edge, then glue brace to back of chalkboard and back of head to stabilize head.

9 Thread gold cord through back brace; tie ends in a knot. Glue cord to back of elf to secure. ●

```
COLOR KEY
REINDEER
Worsted Weight Yarn          Yards
☐ Buff #334                      4
■ Warm brown #336                8
  Uncoded areas are brown
  #328 Continental Stitches       1
/ Brown #328 Overcasting
#3 Pearl Cotton
/ Black #310 Backstitch
Color numbers given are for Red Heart
Super Saver worsted weight yarn Art. E301
and DMC #3 pearl cotton.
```

Reindeer Ear
8 holes x 4 holes
Cut 2, reverse 1

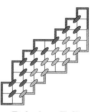

Reindeer Tail
8 holes x 9 holes
Cut 1

Reindeer Hoof
5 holes x 7 holes
Cut 2, reverse 1

Elf Hand
5 holes x 5 holes
Cut 2, reverse 1

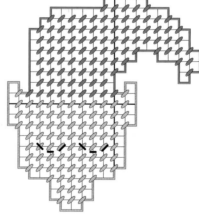

Elf Head
18 holes x 20 holes
Cut 1

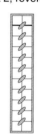

Elf Brace
2 holes x 11 holes
Cut 1

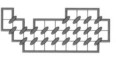

Elf Shoe
10 holes x 4 holes
Cut 2, reverse 1

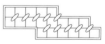

Elf Hat Brim
9 holes x 3 holes
Cut 1

```
COLOR KEY
ELF
Worsted Weight Yarn          Yards
☐ Tan #334                       6
■ Paddy green #686               6
☐ White #3311                    1
#3 Pearl Cotton
/ Black #310 Backstitch and Straight Stitch
Color numbers given are for Red Heart Classic worsted
weight yarn Art. E267, Red Heart Jeweltones worsted
weight yarn Art. E278 and DMC #3 pearl cotton.
```

Musical Ball

Design by Angie Arickx

Add a musical touch to your tree

Intermediate
Skill Level

Create this special ornament for the musician in your family. A golden French horn adorned with holly is tucked inside this sparkling ball as a musical accent.

Materials

- ☐ 2 (5") plastic canvas hexagons by Uniek
- ☐ Uniek Needloft plastic canvas yarn as listed in color key
- ☐ ⅛"-wide Plastic Canvas 7 Metallic Needlepoint Yarn by Rainbow Gallery as listed in color key
- ☐ #16 tapestry needle
- ☐ 12 (3mm) red pompoms
- ☐ Miniature French horn ornament
- ☐ Hot-glue gun

Instructions

1 Following graphs (page 34), cut two ball sections and four holly leaf pieces from plastic canvas hexagons, cutting away gray areas .

2 Stitch pieces following graphs. Overlap shaded blue areas at ends of the two ball sections together while stitching, forming a ball.

3 Overcast inside edges of ball with gold. Overcast holly leaves with holly.

4 Glue three red pompoms to each holly leaf following graph. Using photo as a guide through step 6, glue two holly pieces to top of ball. Glue one holly piece to each side of French horn.

5 Thread a 10" length of gold needlepoint yarn through hole in French horn and knot about ¼" above horn.

6 Place horn and yarn inside ball. Thread yarn ends through two holes in top of ball; tie ends in a knot to form a loop for hanging. ●

Continued on page 34

Star of Bethlehem

Design by Angie Arickx

"Silent night, holy night"

Advanced
Skill Level

Remember the miracle of Jesus' birth with this glistening ornament reminiscent of the beautiful Star of Bethlehem.

Materials

- ☐ 1 sheet 10-count plastic canvas
- ☐ 1⁄16"-wide Plastic Canvas 10 Metallic Needlepoint Yarn by Rainbow Gallery as listed in color key
- ☐ #18 tapestry needle

Instructions

1 Cut and stitch 24 star points according to graph (page 34).

2 Divide stitched pieces into eight groups of three. With right sides facing, Whipstitch one group of three together along straight edges, forming a three-pointed section. Center point of section is at blue dot on graph. Repeat with remaining seven groups.

3 Working with four sections and following Fig. 1, with wrong sides together, Whipstitch point A on section 1 to point B on section 2. Whipstitch point B on section 1 to point A on section 3.

4 Whipstitch point A of section 2 to point B of section 4 and point B of section 3 to point A of section 4, completing one half of star.

5 Repeat with remaining four sections to make second half of star.

6 Matching edges of points C, Whipstitch wrong sides of two halves together. ●

COLOR KEY
☐ Section 1
☐ Section 2
☐ Section 3
☐ Section 4

Fig. 1

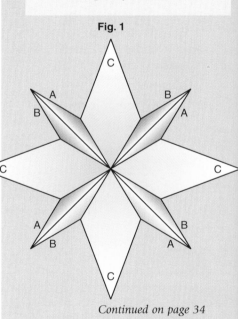

Continued on page 34

Jingle Bell Stars

Designs by Vicki Blizzard

Oh, what fun these jingling bells are!

Snowman

Cutting & Stitching

1 Cut face, hat and nose pieces from plastic canvas according to graphs (page 20). Do not cut star shape.

2 Stitch each section of star following pattern given on graph; Overcast with white pearlized metallic cord.

3 Stitch face, hat and nose pieces following graphs, reversing one nose piece before stitching.

Overcast face with white and hat with black. Whipstitch wrong sides of nose pieces together with orange.

Assembly

1 Glue royal blue felt to back of stitched star with hot glue. Let dry. Trim felt to fit.

2 Using jewel glue, attach five of the crystal rhinestones to star where indicated on graph.

3 Using photo as a guide throughout assembly, center

and hot-glue nose to face between cheeks. Attach cabochons to face for mouth and eyes with jewel glue.

4 Wrap a 3" piece of plaid ribbon around front of hat and hot-glue ends to backside. With jewel glue, attach snowflake to ribbon on left side of hat, then attach remaining rhinestone to center of snowflake.

5 Using needle-nose pliers, attach one jump ring to each white jingle bell, then attach one jump ring with bell to each point of star where indicated on graph.

Jingle Bell Stars

Beginner
Skill Level

Santa and Mr. Snowman will be the stars of Christmas as you hang these jingling character ornaments together on your tree!

Materials

Snowman

- ☐ 1 plastic canvas star shape by Uniek
- ☐ Small amount 7-count plastic canvas
- ☐ Spinrite plastic canvas yarn as listed in color key
- ☐ Darice Bright Pearls pearlized metallic cord as listed in color key
- ☐ #16 tapestry needle
- ☐ 6 (4mm) crystal Austrian glass rhinestones #110-626-01 from National Artcraft
- ☐ 7 (5mm) round black cabochons #X550-052 from The Beadery
- ☐ 5 (⅝") white jingle bells
- ☐ 5 (7mm) gold jump rings
- ☐ Needle-nose pliers
- ☐ Mill Hill Products white metal snowflake #15001 from Gay Bowles Sales, Inc.

Continued on page 21

6 Using hot glue throughout, center and attach face to star. Glue hat to face at an angle. Tie remaining ribbon in a small bow; trim ends. Glue bow to star at left bottom of face.

7 Cut a 12" length of white pearl cord. Attach to top point of star with a Lark's Head Knot (Fig. 1). Tie ends in a knot to form a loop for hanging.

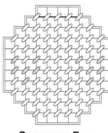

**Fig. 1
Lark's Head Knot**

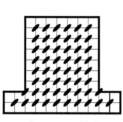

Snowman Hat
11 holes x 9 holes
Cut 1

Snowman Face
10 holes x 11 holes
Cut 1

Santa
Cutting & Stitching

1 Cut head, mustache, hat and hat dangle from plastic canvas according to graphs. Do not cut star shape.

2 Stitch each section of star following pattern given on graph (page 21); Overcast with gold cord.

3 Stitch head, mustache, hat and hat dangle following graphs. When background stitching is completed, work white Straight Stitches for eyebrows on head.

4 Overcast head, mustache and fur trim on hat with white. Overcast remaining side edges of hat with wine, leaving top edge unstitched. Overcast around sides

COLOR KEY	
SNOWMAN	
Plastic Canvas Yarn	**Yards**
☐ White #0001	2
☐ Pale pink #0003	½
■ Royal #0026	13
■ Black #0028	2
☐ Orange #0030	1
Pearlized Metallic Cord	
⬦ White #3410-01 Overcasting	2
● Attach crystal rhinestone	
○ Attach jump ring	
Color numbers given are for Spinrite plastic canvas yarn and Darice Bright Pearls Cord.	

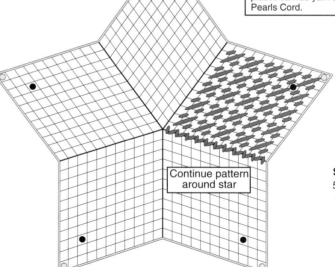

Continue pattern around star

Snowman Base
Stitch 1

Snowman Nose
5 holes x 2 holes
Cut 2, reverse 1

Jingle Bell Stars

Materials

Continued from page 20

- 12" of ⅜"-wide MacKenzie tartan plaid ribbon #222 791-242 from Wrights
- 6" x 6" piece royal blue felt
- Crafter's Pick Jewel Bond glue from Adhesive Products Inc.
- Hot-glue gun

Santa

- 1 plastic canvas star shape by Uniek
- Small amount 7-count plastic canvas
- Spinrite plastic canvas yarn as listed in color key
- Darice Bright Jewels metallic cord as listed in color key
- #16 tapestry needle
- 5 (4mm) ruby Austrian glass rhinestones #110-636-09 from National Artcraft
- 2 (5mm) round black cabochons #X550-052 from The Beadery
- 6mm round transparent ruby bead #705-017 from The Beadery
- 5 (⅝") gold jingle bells
- 5 (7mm) gold jump rings
- Needle-nose pliers
- 2" x 3" piece white felt
- 6" x 6" piece green felt
- Crafter's Pick Jewel Bond glue from Adhesive Products Inc.
- Hot-glue gun

and tip of hat dangle with wine, leaving top edge unstitched.

5 Place wrong side of hat dangle on right side of hat and Whip-stitch top edges together with wine.

Assembly

1 With hot glue, glue white felt to backside of Santa head and green felt to backside of star. Let dry. Trim felt to fit.

2 Using jewel glue, attach the five ruby rhinestones to star where indicated on graph. Glue black cabochons for eyes and ruby bead for nose to head where indicated on graph.

3 Using needle-nose pliers, attach one jump ring to each gold jingle bell, then attach one jump ring with bell to each point of star where indicated on graph.

4 Using photo as a guide throughout assembly, center and hot-glue head to star; glue mustache under nose and hat to top of head.

5 Cut a 12" length of gold metallic cord. Attach to top point of star with a Lark's Head Knot (Fig. 1). Tie ends in a knot to form a loop for hanging. ●

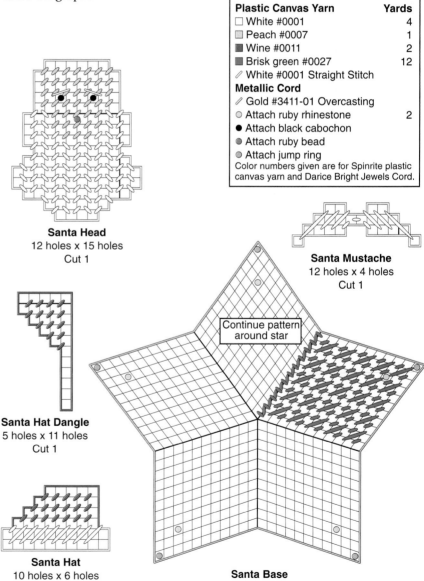

COLOR KEY	
SANTA	
Plastic Canvas Yarn	**Yards**
☐ White #0001	4
▨ Peach #0007	1
▩ Wine #0011	2
▧ Brisk green #0027	12
✐ White #0001 Straight Stitch	
Metallic Cord	
✐ Gold #3411-01 Overcasting	
○ Attach ruby rhinestone	2
● Attach black cabochon	
● Attach ruby bead	
○ Attach jump ring	
Color numbers given are for Spinrite plastic canvas yarn and Darice Bright Jewels Cord.	

Santa Head
12 holes x 15 holes
Cut 1

Santa Mustache
12 holes x 4 holes
Cut 1

Santa Hat Dangle
5 holes x 11 holes
Cut 1

Continue pattern around star

Santa Hat
10 holes x 6 holes
Cut 1

Santa Base
Stitch 1

Snow Crystals

Designs by Vicki Blizzard

Peace and goodwill to all!

Beginner
Skill Level

As they sparkle and shine on your tree, this trio of ornaments will bring you and yours a message of peace and goodwill.

Materials

- ¼ sheet Uniek Quick-Count 10-count plastic canvas
- DMC #3 pearl cotton as listed in color key
- Kreinik Medium (#16) Braid as listed in color key
- Kreinik Fine (#8) Braid as listed in color key
- #22 tapestry needle
- 3 acrylic snowflake shapes #30460 from Daniel Enterprises
- Ceramcoat Sparkle Glaze from Delta Technical Coatings
- Small paintbrush
- Scribbles 3-D Fabric Writers paint from Duncan Enterprises:
  Glittering crystal #SC 301
  Glittering ruby #SC 307
  Glittering emerald #SC 313
- ½ yard each of ⅛"-wide

- royal blue, red and green satin ribbon
- ☐ 50 (2½ mm) Aurora crystal Austrian glass rhinestones #110-565-04 from National Artcraft
- ☐ Crafter's Pick Jewel Bond glue from Adhesive Products Inc.

Instructions

1 Cut plastic canvas according to graphs below.

2 Stitch pieces following graphs, working entire background on Joy insert with Christmas red, entire background on Peace insert with dark royal blue and entire background on Noel insert with very dark emerald green.

3 Over completed Continental Stitches, work Cross Stitches with pearl medium (#16) braid and Backstitches and Straight Stitches with pearl fine (#8) braid. Overcast each insert with pearl medium (#16) braid.

4 Remove and discard acrylic backs and vinyl-weave inserts from snowflakes.

5 Paint wrong side of snowflakes, except recessed centers, with two coats of sparkle glaze, drying thoroughly between coats. Outline center circle and all other openings on snowflakes, except hanger hole, with fabric paint, making one snowflake of each color.

6 Glue rhinestones to stitched inserts where indicated on graphs. Glue remaining rhinestones to acrylic snowflakes where indicated on Fig. 1.

7 Glue matching colored stitched insert inside recessed opening of each snowflake.

8 Attach matching ribbon to hanger hole with a Lark's Head Knot (Fig. 2). Tie ends in a secure knot 2" from snowflake, then tie ends in a small bow; trim as desired. Secure bows with a drop of jewel glue on wrong sides of knots. ●

Fig. 1

Fig. 2
Lark's Head Knot

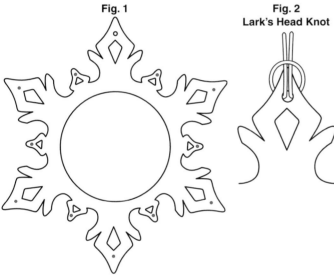

COLOR KEY	
#3 Pearl Cotton	**Yards**
Uncoded background on joy insert is Christmas red #321 Continental Stitches	5
Uncoded background on peace insert is dark royal blue #796 Continental Stitches	5
Uncoded background on noel insert is very dark emerald green #909 Continental Stitches	5
Medium (#16) Braid	
✎ Pearl #032 Cross Stitch and Overcasting	6
Fine (#8) Braid	
✎ Pearl #032 Backstitch and Straight Stitch	6
● Attach crystal rhinestone	
Color numbers given are for DMC #3 pearl cotton and Kreinik Medium (#16) Braid and Fine (#8) Braid.	

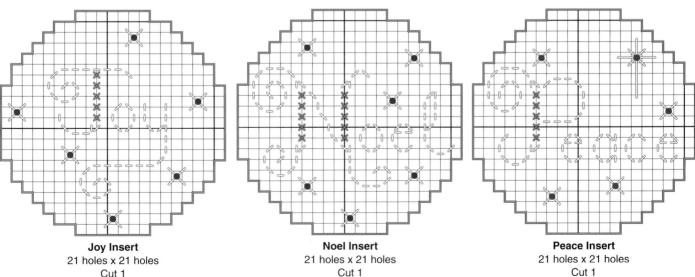

Joy Insert
21 holes x 21 holes
Cut 1

Noel Insert
21 holes x 21 holes
Cut 1

Peace Insert
21 holes x 21 holes
Cut 1

Winter Birdhouses

Designs by Celia Lange Designs

Three sweet ornaments to add to your tree

A Festival of Trees

Beginner
Skill Level

Invite three miniature birds to nest in your Christmas tree with this set of charming birdhouse ornaments!

Materials

- ☐ 2 sheets Darice Ultra Stiff 7-count plastic canvas
- ☐ Coats & Clark Red Heart Super Saver worsted weight yarn Art. E301 as listed in color key
- ☐ DMC #3 pearl cotton as listed in color key
- ☐ #16 tapestry needle
- ☐ 3 rounded-end toothpicks
- ☐ 3 (1"–1½"-long) resin birds (samples used red, blue and brown)
- ☐ Needle-nose pliers (optional)
- ☐ Hot-glue gun

Instructions

1 Cut plastic canvas according to graphs (pages 25 and 26).

2 Stitch pieces following graphs, reversing back for green birdhouse before stitching. Work uncoded areas on birdhouse fronts, backs and sides with colors indicated in color key. Stitch backs without black holes, filling in with Continental Stitch color indicated.

3 When background stitching is completed, work white pearl cotton Backstitches. Following graphs for all Whipstitching and Overcasting, Whipstitch front, back and sides of each birdhouse together, easing pieces together on burgundy birdhouse.

4 Work black pearl cotton Straight Stitches at top of each checked pattern, wrapping a stitch around each corner.

5 Whipstitch bottoms to corresponding birdhouses; Overcast top edges of houses. Work remaining black pearl cotton Straight Stitches at bottom of each checked pattern on front, back and sides as in step 4, using needle-nose pliers if desired.

6 Overcast green birdhouse roof. For hanger, cut desired length of yarn and insert ends from top to bottom through center hole of roof. Knot ends together on wrong side; glue to secure.

7 Whipstitch top edges of burgundy roof pieces together and

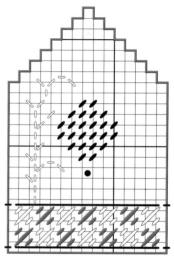

Blue Birdhouse Front & Back
15 holes x 23 holes
Cut 2
Do not stitch black hole on back
Replace with skipper blue

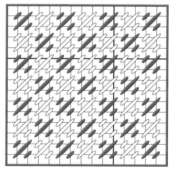

Blue Birdhouse Roof
15 holes x 15 holes
Cut 2

COLOR KEY	
Worsted Weight Yarn	**Yards**
☐ White #311	18
■ Black #312	3
■ Dark spruce #361	38
■ Burgundy #376	44
■ Skipper blue #384	42
Uncoded areas on green birdhouse pieces are dark spruce #361 Continental Stitches	
Uncoded areas on burgundy birdhouse pieces are burgundy #376 Continental Stitches	
Uncoded areas on blue birdhouse pieces are skipper blue #384 Continental Stitches	
#3 Pearl Cotton	
⁄ White Backstitch	
✓ Black #310 Straight Stitch	
● Attach toothpick perch	
Color numbers given are for Red Heart Super Saver worsted weight yarn Art. E301 and DMC #3 pearl cotton.	

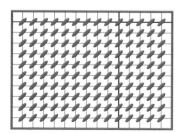

Blue Birdhouse Bottom
15 holes x 11 holes
Cut 1

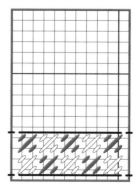

Blue Birdhouse Side
11 holes x 16 holes
Cut 2

Winter Birdhouses

8 Cut toothpicks 2¼"–2½" long. Insert one toothpick through hole on each front where indicated on graphs; glue to back. Center and glue roofs over birdhouses. Glue one bird to toothpick perch on each birdhouse. ●

blue roof pieces together, leaving a hanging loop in center of each peak. Overcast remaining edges.

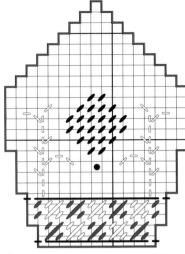

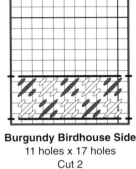

Burgundy Birdhouse Front & Back
17 holes x 23 holes
Cut 2
Do not stitch black hole on back
Replace with burgundy

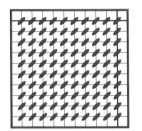

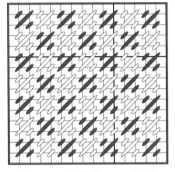

Burgundy Birdhouse Bottom
11 holes x 11 holes
Cut 1

Burgundy Birdhouse Roof
15 holes x 15 holes
Cut 2

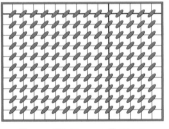

Burgundy Birdhouse Side
11 holes x 17 holes
Cut 2

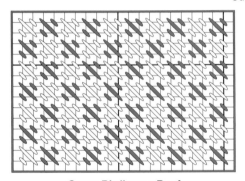

Green Birdhouse Roof
21 holes x 15 holes
Cut 1

Green Birdhouse Bottom
15 holes x 11 holes
Cut 1

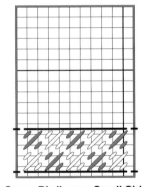

Green Birdhouse Small Side
11 holes x 16 holes
Cut 1

COLOR KEY

Worsted Weight Yarn	Yards
□ White #311	18
■ Black #312	3
■ Dark spruce #361	38
■ Burgundy #376	44
■ Skipper blue #384	42

Uncoded areas on green birdhouse pieces are dark spruce #361 Continental Stitches
Uncoded areas on burgundy birdhouse pieces are burgundy #376 Continental Stitches
Uncoded areas on blue birdhouse pieces are skipper blue #384 Continental Stitches

#3 Pearl Cotton
⁄ White Backstitch
⁄ Black #310 Straight Stitch
● Attach toothpick perch

Color numbers given are for Red Heart Super Saver worsted weight yarn Art. E301 and DMC #3 pearl cotton.

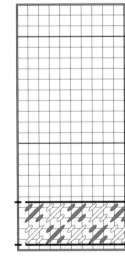

Green Birdhouse Large Side
11 holes x 23 holes
Cut 1

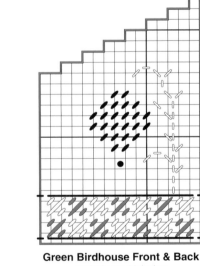

Green Birdhouse Front & Back
15 holes x 23 holes
Cut 2, reverse 1
Do not stitch black hole on back
Replace with dark spruce

75 Merry Christmas Projects in Plastic Canvas

Hearts Come Home Ornament

Design by Celia Lange Designs

Home for the holidays

Beginner
Skill Level

Welcome family and friends into your home during the holidays with this heartwarming ornament.

Materials

- ☐ ¼ sheet Darice Ultra Stiff 7-count plastic canvas
- ☐ Coats & Clark Red Heart Classic worsted weight yarn Art. E267 as listed in color key
- ☐ Coats & Clark Red Heart Super Saver worsted weight yarn Art. E301 as listed in color key
- ☐ DMC #3 pearl cotton as listed in color key
- ☐ #16 tapestry needle
- ☐ ¾" dark red or burgundy heart button
- ☐ Hot-glue gun

Instructions

1 Cut and stitch plastic canvas according to graphs (page 29).

2 Stitch and Overcast pieces following graphs. When background stitching and Overcasting are completed, work Backstitches, then French Knots.

3 Using photo as a guide, center and sew heart button to house with medium garnet pearl cotton.

4 For hanger, cut one 6" length of medium garnet pearl cotton. Fold length in half and thread ends through stitches on center top backside house, leaving a 1½" loop. Glue ends to secure.

5 Glue roof to house. ●

Continued on page 29

Baby's First Christmas

Design by Mary T. Cosgrove

A memory ornament for your little one

Instructions

1 Cut plastic canvas according to graphs (pages 28 and 29).

2 Stitch pieces following graphs, working uncoded background on sides and sole with white Continental Stitches.

3 When background stitching is completed, work green ribbon Straight Stitches for leaves. With red ribbon, Backstitch letters on sole and add French Knot berries to sides, wrapping ribbon around needle twice.

4 Using white through step 5, Overcast inside edges on sides. With wrong sides facing throughout, Whipstitch sides to back at holes indicated with yellow dots.

5 Whipstitch tongue of bootie to corresponding edges indicated with blue dots. Whipstitch sole to bottom edges of sides and back. Overcast remaining edges.

6 Thread ends of red satin ribbon from back to front through cutout holes on sides. Tie ribbon in a small bow, centering in front. With sewing needle and nylon thread, tack jingle bell to center of bow.

7 Cut desired length of nylon thread and thread through center top hole of tongue. Tie ends in a knot to form a loop for hanging. ●

COLOR KEY	
Plastic Canvas Yarn	**Yards**
☐ White #41	10
Uncoded areas on sides and sole are white #41 Continental Stitches	
⅛" Ribbon	
✎ Red #003 Backstitch	1
✎ Green #008 Straight Stitch	1
● Red #003 French Knot	
Color numbers given are for Uniek Needloft plastic canvas yarn and Kreinik ⅛" Ribbon.	

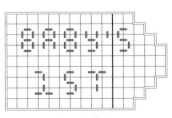

Bootie Sole
15 holes x 9 holes
Cut 1

Beginner
Skill Level

Celebrate your precious little one's first Christmas by stitching him or her a tiny Christmas bootie to hang on the tree! When the holiday is over, be sure to save the bootie in your child's hope chest!

Materials

- ☐ ¼ sheet 7-count Uniek Quick-Count plastic canvas
- ☐ Uniek Needloft plastic canvas yarn as listed in color key
- ☐ Kreinik ⅛" Ribbon as listed in color key
- ☐ #16 tapestry needle
- ☐ 12" of ³⁄₁₆"-wide picot-edge red satin ribbon
- ☐ 10mm gold jingle bell
- ☐ Sewing needle and nylon monofilament thread

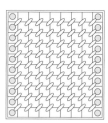

Bootie Back
9 holes x 10 holes
Cut 1

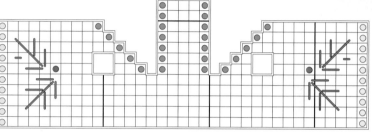

Bootie Sides
35 holes x 12 holes
Cut 1

Hearts Come Home Ornament

Continued from page 27

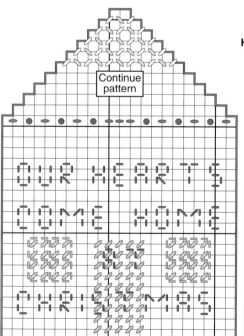

Hearts Come Home House
22 holes x 31 holes
Cut 1

Hearts Come Home Roof
21 holes x 21 holes
Cut 1

COLOR KEY	
Worsted Weight Yarn	**Yards**
☐ White #311	6
☐ Aran #313	6
☐ Cornmeal #320	1
☐ Light sage #631	2
☐ Dark sage #633	7
╱ Light sage #631 Backstitch	
#3 Pearl Cotton	
╱ Medium garnet #815 Backstitch	5
● Medium garnet #815 French Knot	
Color numbers given are for Red Heart Classic worsted weight yarn Art. E267, Red Heart Super Saver worsted weight yarn Art E301 and DMC #3 pearl cotton.	

Holiday Seed Packets

Designs by Celia Lange Designs

Plant a packet of holiday love

Instructions

1 Cut plastic canvas according to graphs (page 31).

2 Stitch pieces following graphs, working uncoded area on seed packets with light sage Continental Stitches and uncoded background on banners with cornmeal Continental Stitches.

3 Overcast seed packets with burgundy and banners with dark sage. Backstitch letters with black pearl cotton.

4 Using photo as a guide, glue banners and corresponding flowers and miniatures to packets.

5 For hangers, cut desired length burgundy yarn for each packet. Fold lengths in half and thread ends through stitches on center top backsides of seed packets, leaving 1"–1½" loops. Glue ends to secure. ●

Beginner
Skill Level

Plant a bouquet of holiday flowers in your mind with three attractive seed packet ornaments accented with a sprig of holly, a pine bough and a poinsettia.

Materials

- [ ] 1 sheet Darice Ultra Stiff 7-count plastic canvas
- [ ] Coats & Clark Red Heart Classic worsted weight yarn Art. E267 as listed in color key
- [ ] Coats & Clark Red Heart Super Saver worsted weight yarn Art. E301 as listed in color key
- [ ] DMC #3 pearl cotton as listed in color key
- [ ] #16 tapestry needle
- [ ] 2 small silk poinsettia flowers
- [ ] 2 lengths miniature pine stems
- [ ] 2 miniature pinecones
- [ ] 3 miniature holly clusters
- [ ] Hot-glue gun

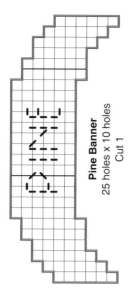

Pine Banner
25 holes x 10 holes
Cut 1

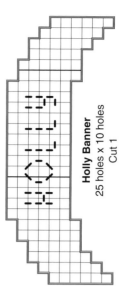

Holly Banner
25 holes x 10 holes
Cut 1

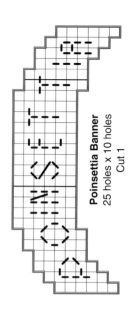

Poinsettia Banner
25 holes x 10 holes
Cut 1

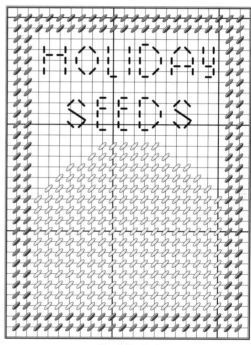

Seed Packet
23 holes x 31 holes
Cut 3

COLOR KEY

Worsted Weight Yarn	Yards
☐ Aran #313	15
■ Burgundy #376	11
■ Dark sage #633	12
Uncoded areas on banners are cornmeal #320 Continental Stitches	8
Uncoded areas on seed packets are light sage #631 Continental Stitches	14

#3 Pearl Cotton
✎ Black #310 Backstitch

Color numbers given are for Red Heart Classic worsted weight yarn Art. E267, Red Heart Super Saver worsted weight yarn Art. E301 and DMC #3 pearl cotton.

"Dear Santa"

Designs by Celia Lange Designs

Children will love this pair of ornaments

A Festival of Trees

Beginner
Skill Level

Capture the excitement of writing to Santa and sending letters to the North Pole with this pair of colorful ornaments.

Materials

- ☐ 1 sheet 7-count plastic canvas
- ☐ Coats & Clark Red Heart Classic worsted weight yarn Art. E267 as listed in color key
- ☐ DMC #3 pearl cotton as listed in color key
- ☐ #16 tapestry needle
- ☐ 3½" x 3" piece white paper
- ☐ 2 lengths miniature pine stems
- ☐ 4 miniature white-tipped pinecones
- ☐ 6 small red berries
- ☐ Hot-glue gun

Instructions

1 Cut plastic canvas according to graphs (pages 33 and 34).

2 Stitch pieces following graphs, reversing one red envelope side flap before stitching. Work uncoded area on green envelope with paddy green Continental Stitches and uncoded background on stamp with white Continental Stitches.

3 Overcast green envelope with paddy green and stamp with white. Work embroidery on stamp and green envelope with pearl cotton when background stitching and Overcasting are completed.

4 Using cherry red throughout for red envelope, Overcast top flap of envelope back from dot to dot, side and top edges of bottom flap from dot to dot and all but the long straight edge on side flaps.

5 Placing wrong side of flaps on right side of back, Whipstitch straight edges on side flaps to side edges of back, then Whipstitch bottom edges of bottom flap and back together.

6 Write a letter to Santa on white paper, trimming to fit if necessary. Using photo as a guide through step 9, place letter on back and glue in place. Bring sides in, then bring up bottom flap; glue in place.

7 For hangers, cut one 4½"–5" length each of paddy green and cherry red yarn. Fold lengths in half and thread ends of corresponding colors through stitches on center top backsides of envelopes, leaving 1½" loops. Glue ends to secure.

8 For green envelope, glue stamp in place. Glue two pinecones and four berries to lower left corner.

9 For red envelope, center and glue pine stems and remaining pine-cones and berries to bottom flap. ●

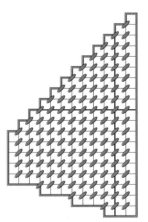

Red Envelope Side Flap
12 holes x 19 holes
Cut 2, reverse 1

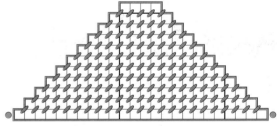

Red Envelope Bottom Flap
24 holes x 11 holes
Cut 1

Stamp
4 holes x 5 holes
Cut 1

COLOR KEY	
Worsted Weight Yarn	**Yards**
☐ White #1	3
■ Cherry red #912	16
Uncoded area on stamp is white #1 Continental Stitches	
Uncoded area on green envelope is paddy green #686 Continental Stitches	10
✎ Paddy green #686 Overcasting	
#3 Pearl Cotton	
✎ White Backstitch and Straight Stitch	2
✎ Bright Christmas green #700 Backstitch	1
● Christmas red #321 French Knot	1
Color numbers given are for Red Heart Classic worsted weight yarn Art. E267 and DMC #3 pearl cotton.	

"Dear Santa"

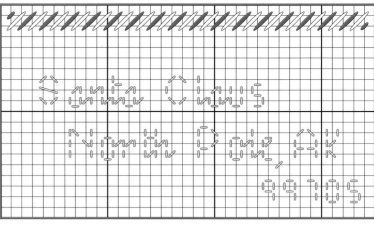

Green Envelope
35 holes x 20 holes
Cut 1

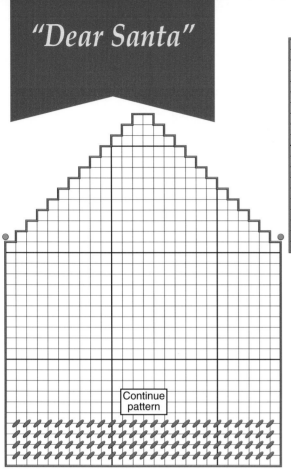

Continue pattern

Red Envelope Back
26 holes x 33 holes
Cut 1

COLOR KEY

Worsted Weight Yarn	Yards
☐ White #1	3
■ Cherry red #912	16
Uncoded area on stamp is white #1 Continental Stitches	
Uncoded area on green envelope is paddy green #686 Continental Stitches	10
⁄ Paddy green #686 Overcasting	
#3 Pearl Cotton	
⁄ White Backstitch and Straight Stitch	2
⁄ Bright Christmas green #700 Backstitch	1
● Christmas red #321 French Knot	1

Color numbers given are for Red Heart Classic worsted weight yarn Art. E267 and DMC #3 pearl cotton.

Musical Ball

Continued from page 17

COLOR KEY

Plastic Canvas Yarn	Yards
■ Christmas red #02	6
■ Holly #27	4
⅛" Metallic Needlepoint Yarn	
☐ Gold #PC1	6
● Attach red pompom	

Color numbers given are for Uniek Needloft plastic canvas yarn and Rainbow Gallery Plastic Canvas 7 Metallic Needlepoint Yarn.

Ball Section
Cut 2
Holly Leaves
Cut 4

Star of Bethlehem

Continued from page 18

Star Point
12 holes x 12 holes
Cut 24

COLOR KEY

¹⁄₁₆ Metallic Needlepoint Yarn	Yards
☐ White pearl #PM70	24

Color number given is for Rainbow Gallery Plastic Canvas 10 Metallic Needlepoint Yarn.

Quick & Easy Gifts

Each of the gifts in this colorful collection can be stitched from start to finish in just several hours. So as the stitching days until Christmas wind down, you'll still have time to stitch these last-minute goodies.

Festive Frames

Designs by Kimberly A. Suber

Fun frames anyone will love to have

Cut plastic canvas according to graphs (pages 37 and 38).

Instructions

1 Cut plastic canvas according to graphs (pages 37 and 38). Cut one 15-hole x 27-hole piece for poinsettia frame stand and one 13-hole x 27-hole piece for holly wreath frame stand. Frame backs and stands will remain unstitched.

2 Stitch frame fronts, poinsettia petals and poinsettia center following graphs. Overcast holly leaves with green, then work red French Knots.

3 Overcast poinsettia petals and poinsettia center with adjacent colors. Overcast inside edges of frame fronts with gold cord.

4 Whipstitch frame stands to frame backs where indicated on graphs using green for poinsettia frame and red for holly wreath frame.

5 Whipstitch wrong sides of poinsettia frame front and back together with green. Whipstitch wrong sides of holly wreath frame front and back together with red.

6 Using photo as a guide through step 7, glue holly leaves together in a circle, overlapping ends. Tie a 6" length of gold cord in a bow, trimming ends as desired; glue to top of wreath. Glue wreath to lower left corner of frame front, making sure bottom edges are even.

7 Glue poinsettia petals together so that four top petals are evenly spaced between four bot-

Quick & Easy Gifts

Beginner
Skill Level

Very quick and easy to stitch, this pair of frames makes a pretty and practical gift for those "hard to shop for" people on your gift list.

Materials

- ☐ 2 sheets 7-count plastic canvas
- ☐ Worsted weight yarn as listed in color key
- ☐ Metallic cord as listed in color key
- ☐ #16 tapestry needle
- ☐ Hot-glue gun

tom petals. Glue poinsettia center to center of petals. Glue assembled poinsettia to lower left corner of frame front, making sure bottom edges are even. ●

Poinsettia Center
4 holes x 4 holes
Cut 1

Poinsettia Petal
3 holes x 5 holes
Cut 8

COLOR KEY	
POINSETTIA FRAME	
Worsted Weight Yarn	**Yards**
■ Green	9
■ Red	3
☐ Yellow	1
Metallic Cord	
■ Gold	8
╱ Attach frame stand	

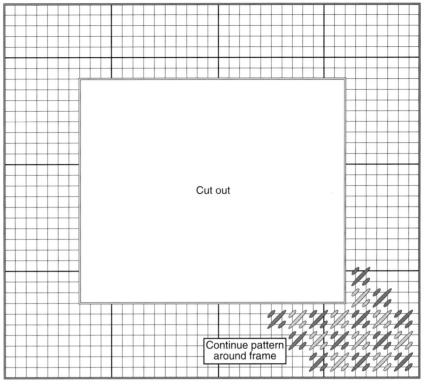

Poinsettia Frame Front
39 holes x 35 holes
Cut 1

Cut out

Continue pattern around frame

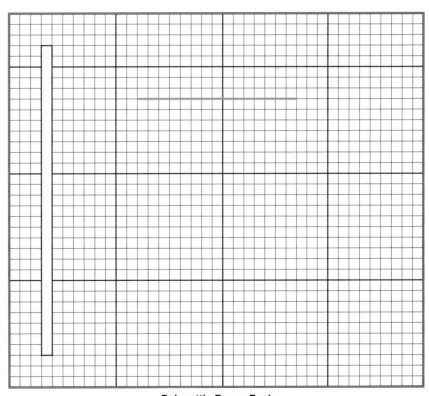

Poinsettia Frame Back
39 holes x 35 holes
Cut 1
Do not stitch

Festive Frames

Holly Leaf
3 holes x 5 holes
Cut 7

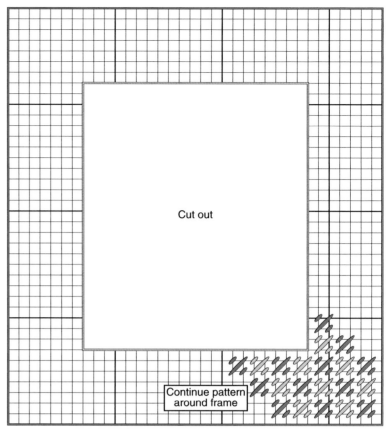

Cut out

Continue pattern around frame

Holly Wreath Frame Front
35 holes x 39 holes
Cut 1

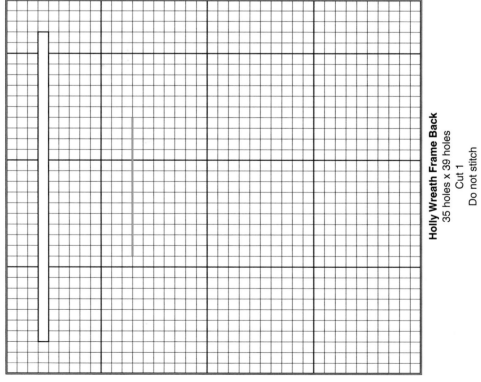

Holly Wreath Frame Back
35 holes x 39 holes
Cut 1
Do not stitch

Christmas Tree Marble Game

Design by Vicki Blizzard

Keep kids busy and happy with a fun game

Christmas Tree Marble Game

Intermediate
Skill Level

Keep youngsters occupied during the car trip to Grandma's house with this festive Christmas game.

Materials

- [ ] 1 sheet Uniek Quick-Count clear 7-count plastic canvas
- [ ] ½ sheet Uniek Quick-Count red 7-count plastic canvas
- [ ] Uniek Needloft plastic canvas yarn as listed in color key
- [ ] #16 tapestry needle
- [ ] Sewing needle and clear thread
- [ ] 8 (6mm) ruby round faceted beads from The Beadery
- [ ] 6" square clear acrylic plastic sheet
- [ ] 6 (14mm) assorted round glass marbles from Mega Marbles by Vacor USA
- [ ] 5¾" square white felt
- [ ] 4 (⅝") pieces of ⅛"-diameter wooden dowel
- [ ] Silicone glue
- [ ] Hot-glue gun

Cutting & Stitching

1 Cut one game board front, one game box top, four game box sides and eight holly leaves from clear plastic canvas according to graphs (pages 40 and 41).

2 Cut one 41-hole x 41-hole piece from red plastic canvas for game board back. Game board back will remain unstitched.

3 Stitch pieces following graphs, working uncoded area on game board front with white Continental Stitches.

4 Work Straight Stitches, French Knots and Smyrna Cross on game board front and Straight Stitches on holly leaves when background stitching is completed.

COLOR KEY	
Plastic Canvas Yarn	**Yards**
■ Red #02	28
■ Maple #13	1
■ Christmas green #28	11
□ Yellow #57	2
Uncoded area is white #41 Continental Stitches	20
⁄ White #41 Overcasting	
⁄ Red #02 Straight Stitch	
⁄ Christmas green #28 Straight Stitch	
○ Yellow #57 French Knot	
● Attach ruby bead	
Color numbers given are for Uniek Needloft plastic canvas yarn.	

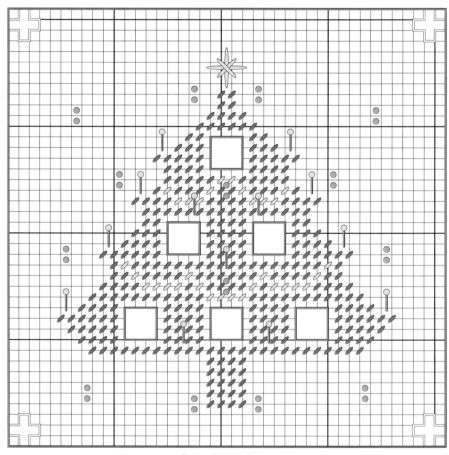

Game Board Front
41 holes x 41 holes
Cut 1 from clear

5 On game board front, Overcast inside edges of tree with Christmas green and inside edges at corner holes with white.

Assembly

1 Place wrong side of game board front on game board back, putting white felt between pieces. With sewing needle and clear thread, tack front to back where indicated with blue dots, pulling all three layers tightly together. Knot thread securely close to stitching on front; trim thread close to knot. Knot will not show.

2 Hot-glue one dowel piece in each corner hole on game

board, making sure dowels stand straight up.

3 Using Christmas red through out assembly, Whipstitch short ends of box sides together, then Whipstitch box top to box sides.

4 Remove protective covering from both sides of acrylic plastic sheet. Run a bead of silicone glue around outside edge of acrylic plastic sheet, applying a small extra amount in each corner; glue in place, centering acrylic plastic sheet over opening on wrong side of game box top.

5 Carefully Whipstitch all but 2" of game board to sides, making sure to catch all layers of board while Whipstitching. Let glue cure

for 24 hours before continuing.

6 When glue is cured, insert marbles through opening and complete Whipstitching.

7 With sewing needle and clear thread, attach one bead to each holly leaf where indicated on graph. Using photo as a guide, glue two leaves to each corner of box top. ●

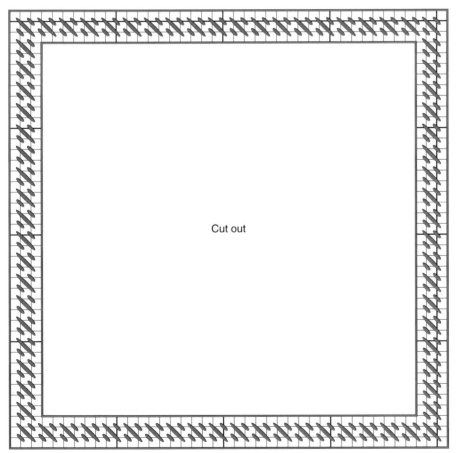

Game Box Top
41 holes x 41 holes
Cut 1 from clear

Holly Leaf
5 holes x 6 holes
Cut 8 from clear

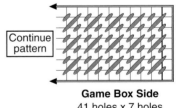

Game Box Side
41 holes x 7 holes
Cut 4 from clear

Holiday Tartan Jewelry

Designs by Vicki Blizzard

Everyone's "mad for plaid" this Christmas

75 Merry Christmas Projects in Plastic Canvas

Quick & Easy Gifts

Intermediate
Skill Level

Tuck this elegant earrings and pin set into Mom's, Sis' or Grandma's stocking to give her a pleasant surprise on Christmas morning!

Materials

- [ ] Small amount Uniek Quick-Count 10-count clear plastic canvas
- [ ] DMC #3 pearl cotton as listed in color key
- [ ] Kreinik Fine (#8) Braid as listed in color key
- [ ] #18 tapestry needle
- [ ] #26 tapestry needle
- [ ] 93 (3mm) round gold beads from The Beadery
- [ ] 13 (9mm) teardrop gold beads with loop
- [ ] 1" round pin back
- [ ] 1 pair earring backs
- [ ] Scraps green felt
- [ ] Hot-glue gun

Instructions

1 Cut two earrings and one pin from plastic canvas according to graphs.

2 Using #18 tapestry needle, stitch pieces following graphs, working gold braid Backstitches over completed background stitching. Overcast all pieces with gold braid, working two stitches in each hole to cover plastic canvas.

3 To attach bead fringe on pin, thread #26 tapestry needle with gold braid. Secure braid on backside near corner hole indicated for attaching bead fringe. Bring needle through corner hole from back to front. Thread nine 3mm gold beads onto braid, then one teardrop gold bead; bring needle

back up through the nine 3mm gold beads.

4 Bring needle from back to front through same hole and repeat beading process as before. Repeat one more time so there are three strands of fringe in corner hole, then repeat twice in each hole indicated on both sides of corner hole.

5 For earrings, using five 3mm gold beads and one teardrop bead for each strand, attach bead fringe in corner hole indicated, following procedure for pin back and making three strands of bead fringe in each earring.

6 Cut felt to fit backs of pin and each earring; glue in place. Glue pin back to top backside of pin and earring backs to top backside of earrings. ●

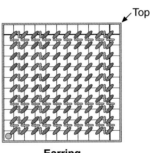

Earring
11 holes x 11 holes
Cut 2

COLOR KEY	
#3 Pearl Cotton	**Yards**
■ Christmas red #321	5
■ Christmas green #699	5
Fine (#8) Braid	
╱ Gold #002HL Backstitch and Overcasting	11
○ Attach bead fringe	
Color numbers given are for DMC #3 pearl cotton and Kreinik Fine (#8) Braid.	

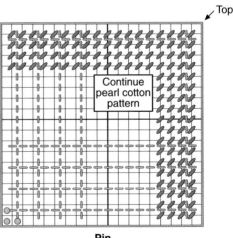

Continue pearl cotton pattern

Pin
19 holes x 19 holes
Cut 1

Santa & Friends Button Covers

Designs by Nancy Marshall

Dress up an outfit in a snap

Project Notes

Button covers used will cover ½" buttons.

Cut floss into 18" lengths. Separate floss, then place strands back together. Use 6 strands for all background stitching and Overcasting. Use 3 strands for Backstitching.

Instructions

1 Cut plastic canvas according to graphs.

2 Stitch each character following graphs and project notes, working uncoded area on reindeer with light brown Continental Stitches, uncoded area on elf with light peach Continental Stitches, uncoded areas on Santa and snowman with white Continental Stitches.

3 Backstitch mouths when back ground stitching is completed. Overcast edges following graphs.

4 Center face area of each char acter over one button cover front, making sure to place stitched design on cover so that bottom of character is at bottom of cover. Glue in place. ●

These darling button covers make delightful stocking stuffers! Stitch a set of four matching covers, or mix and match the four different designs to suit your style.

Materials

- ☐ Small amount 14-count plastic canvas
- ☐ 6-strand embroidery floss as listed in color key
- ☐ #24 tapestry needle
- ☐ 4 (17mm) button covers
- ☐ Craft glue

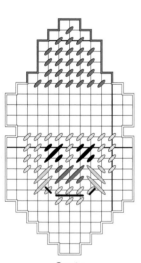

Santa
12 holes x 22 holes
Cut 1

COLOR KEY	
6-Strand Embroidery Floss	**Yards**
■ Black #310	1½
■ Christmas red #321	1
■ Pearl gray #415	½
☐ Dark lemon #444	½
■ Bright Christmas green #700	½
☐ Light rose #3326	½
■ Light brown #434	1½
☐ Light peach #754	1
Uncoded areas on Santa and snowman are white Continental Stitches	2
Uncoded area on reindeer is light brown #434 Continental Stitches	
Uncoded area on elf is light peach #754 Continental Stitches	
⁄ White Overcasting	
⁄ Black #310 Backstitch	
Color numbers given are for DMC 6-strand embroidery floss.	

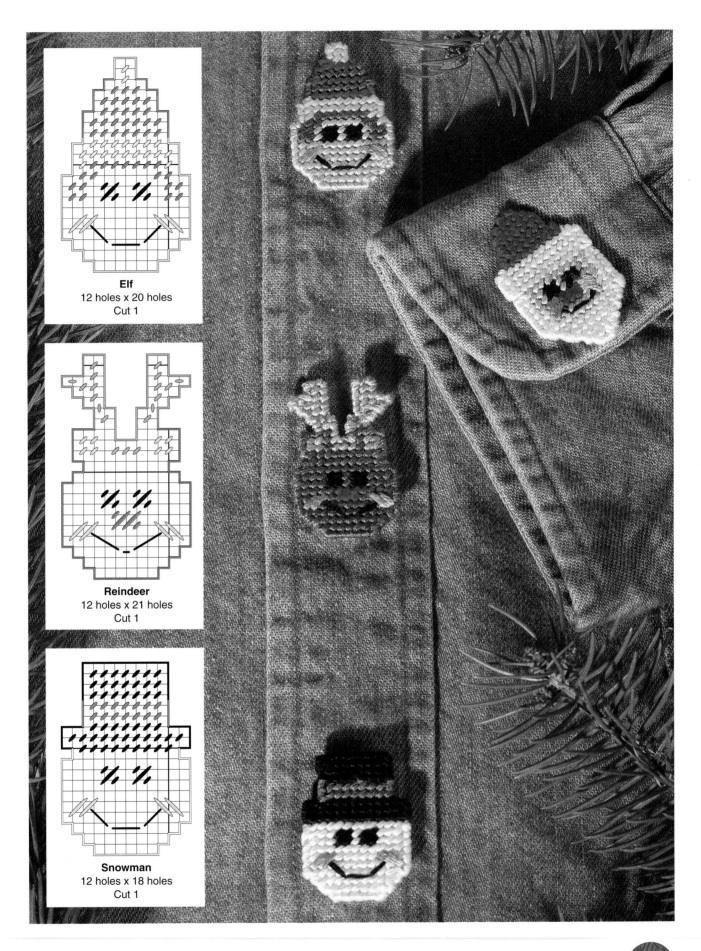

Elf
12 holes x 20 holes
Cut 1

Reindeer
12 holes x 21 holes
Cut 1

Snowman
12 holes x 18 holes
Cut 1

Pet Clocks

Designs by Vicki Blizzard

Pet lovers will adore these whimsical clocks

Pretty Kitty

Instructions

1 Cut head, body front and tail from clear plastic canvas; cut body back and stand from white plastic canvas according to graphs (page 48). Do not cut out hole on body back.

2 Stitch head, body front and tail following graphs, working uncoded areas with straw Reverse Continental Stitches. Body back and stand will remain unstitched.

3 Work Backstitches with 1 ply yarn. For whiskers, thread white embroidery floss from front to back through one of the holes indicated with a blue dot, then thread floss from back to front through second hole indicated with a blue dot.

4 Make ends of floss even on front. Secure floss on back with a drop of glue. Separate ends into individual strands and trim to ½".

5 For tail, Overcast tip with white and remaining edges with yellow. Overcast head with yellow. Do not Overcast edges of opening on body front. With white, Whipstitch long straight edge of stand to backside of unstitched body back where indicated on graph.

6 Set clock to correct time, then insert into opening on body front. Whipstitch wrong sides of body front and back together with yellow.

7 Clip off shanks on eyes with wire cutters. Using photo as a guide, glue eyes to face, then glue head to top of body at an angle.

8 Remove plastic covering from clock face.

Time for a Bone

Instructions

1 Cut body front and back, head, ears and stand pieces from black plastic canvas; cut bone from clear plastic canvas according to graphs (page 48). Do not cut out hole on body back.

2 Stitch head, body front and ears following graphs, reversing one ear before stitching. Stitch and Overcast bone with eggshell. Body back and stand pieces will remain unstitched.

3 Do not Overcast edges of opening on body front. Using black through step 4, Overcast head and ears. Whipstitch long straight edges of stand pieces to backside of unstitched body back where indicated on graph.

4 Set clock to correct time, then insert into opening on body front. Whipstitch wrong sides of body front and back together.

5 Paint backs of eyes with white acrylic paint. Allow to dry. Using wire cutters, clip off shanks.

6 Using photo as a guide throughout, glue eyes in place on head and cabochon for nose to

Intermediate
Skill Level

Here's a perfect gift for your animal-loving friends! Stitch it in colors to match your friend's cat or dog.

Materials

Pretty Kitty

□ ½ sheet Uniek Quick-Count clear 7-count plastic canvas

□ ¼ sheet Uniek Quick-Count pastel white 7-count plastic canvas

□ Uniek Needloft plastic canvas yarn as listed in color key

□ #16 tapestry needle

□ 6" white 6-strand embroidery floss

□ 1⅜" battery-operated mini-clock #908 Arabic from Walnut Hollow Farm Inc.

□ 2 (6mm) brown animal eyes with shanks

□ Wire cutters

□ Hot-glue gun

Continued on page 47

bottom of head. Glue one ear to each side of head front; glue bone to backside of head. Glue head to body at an angle.

7 Remove plastic covering from clock face. ●

Materials

Continued from page 46

Time for a Bone

- ☐ ½ sheet Uniek Quick-Count black 7-count plastic canvas
- ☐ Small amount Uniek Quick-Count clear 7-count plastic canvas
- ☐ Uniek Needloft plastic canvas yarn as listed in color key
- ☐ #16 tapestry needle
- ☐ 6mm round black cabochon from The Beadery
- ☐ 2 (7mm) brown animal eyes with shanks
- ☐ White acrylic paint
- ☐ Paintbrush
- ☐ Wire cutters
- ☐ 1⅜" battery-operated mini-clock #908 Arabic from Walnut Hollow Farm Inc.
- ☐ Hot-glue gun

Pet Clocks

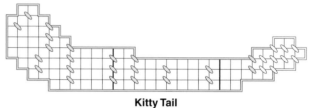

Kitty Clock Stand
7 holes x 22 holes
Cut 1 from white
Do not stitch

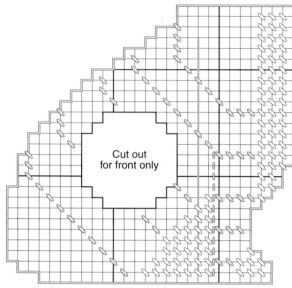

Kitty Body Front & Back
27 holes x 26 holes
Cut 1 front from clear
Stitch as graphed
Cut 1 back from white
Do not stitch

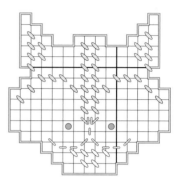

Kitty Head
15 holes x 15 holes
Cut 1 from clear

Kitty Tail
28 holes x 8 holes
Cut 1 front from clear

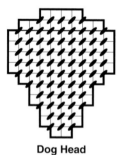

Dog Head
10 holes x 12 holes
Cut 1 from black

Dog Ear
3 holes x 6 holes
Cut 2, reverse 1, from black

Dog Bone
9 holes x 3 holes
Cut 1 from clear

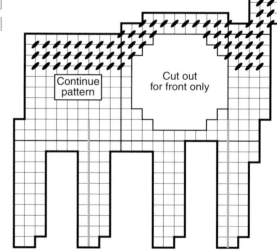

Dog Body Front & Back
25 holes x 32 holes
Cut 2 from black
Do not stitch back

Continue
pattern

Cut out
for front only

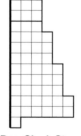

Dog Clock Stand
6 holes x 12 holes
Cut 2 from black

Frame a Christmas Memory

Designs by Alida Macor

Frame your favorite Christmas moments

Frame A Christmas Memory

Beginner
Skill Level

Don't let those beautiful Christmas photos sit in a closet somewhere! Pull out two favorites and display them in these heartwarming frames.

Materials

- ⅔ sheet 10-count plastic canvas
- DMC #3 pearl cotton as listed in color key
- Kreinik Heavy (#32) Braid as listed in color key
- #22 tapestry needle
- 4" x 6" self-standing clear plastic photo frame
- 5" x 7" self-standing clear plastic photo frame
- Craft glue or double-stick tape

Instructions

1 Cut plastic canvas according to graphs.

2 Stitch pieces following graphs, working Running Stitches (Fig. 1) on large frame when background stitching is completed. Overcast inside and outside edges following graphs.

3 Attach stitched frames to fronts of self-standing plastic frames with glue or double-stick tape. ●

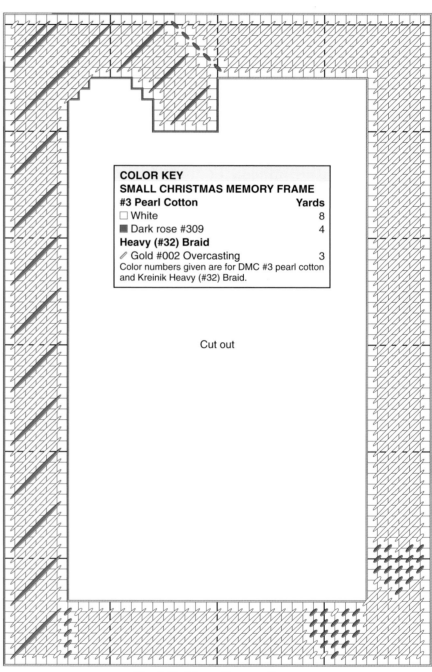

COLOR KEY
SMALL CHRISTMAS MEMORY FRAME

#3 Pearl Cotton	Yards
☐ White	8
■ Dark rose #309	4
Heavy (#32) Braid	
✎ Gold #002 Overcasting	3

Color numbers given are for DMC #3 pearl cotton and Kreinik Heavy (#32) Braid.

Cut out

Small Christmas Memory Frame
40 holes x 61 holes
Cut 1

Fig. 1

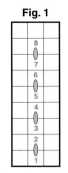

Running Stitch
Bring needle up at 1,
down at 2, up at 3,
down at 4, etc.

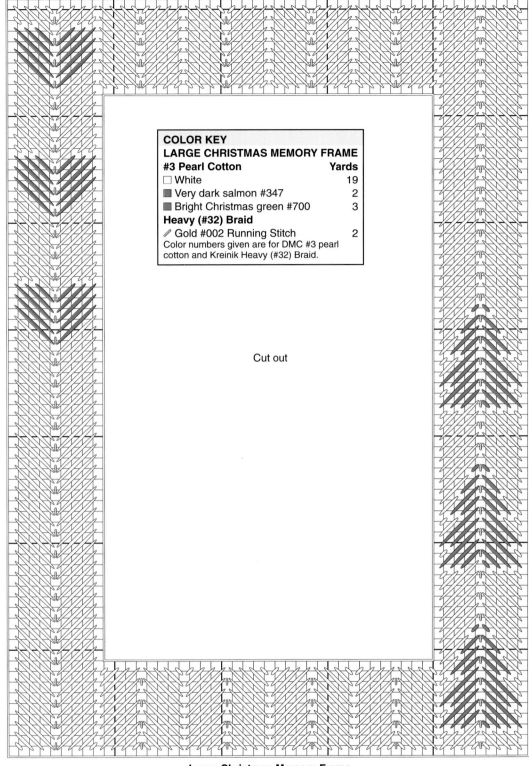

COLOR KEY
LARGE CHRISTMAS MEMORY FRAME

#3 Pearl Cotton	Yards
☐ White	19
◼ Very dark salmon #347	2
◼ Bright Christmas green #700	3

Heavy (#32) Braid

⁄ Gold #002 Running Stitch	2

Color numbers given are for DMC #3 pearl
cotton and Kreinik Heavy (#32) Braid.

Cut out

Large Christmas Memory Frame
49 holes x 71 holes
Cut 1

Christmas Candle Match Holder

Design by Kimberly A. Suber

A pretty matchstick holder

Beginner
Skill Level

Here's a unique gift for someone with a fireplace—a decorative matchstick holder adorned with a poinsettia, candle and dainty French knots.

Materials

- ☐ 1 sheet 7-count plastic canvas
- ☐ Worsted weight yarn as listed in color key
- ☐ #16 tapestry needle
- ☐ Hot-glue gun

Instructions

1 Cut plastic canvas according to graphs.

2 Stitch holder pieces, candle, poinsettia petals and leaves following graphs, working black Straight Stitch on candle and light blue French Knots when background stitching is completed.

3 Using gold, Overcast poinsettia center, then work French Knots. Overcast candle, petals and leaves following graphs.

4 Using royal blue throughout, Whipstitch front, back and sides together, then Whipstitch front, back and sides to bottom. Overcast top edges of holder.

5 Using photo as a guide through step 6, center and glue candle to holder front so that top of flame is above top edge of holder front. Glue two leaves to each side of holder below candle.

6 Place wrong side of one set of petals on right side of second set so that top petals are evenly spaced between bottom petals. Center and glue poinsettia center to top layer of petals, then glue assembled flower between leaves below candle, making sure bottom edges are even. ●

Poinettia Center
5 holes x 5 holes
Cut 1

Poinettia Leaf
5 holes x 9 holes
Cut 4

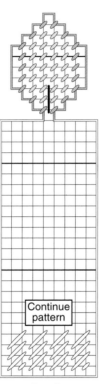

Candle
9 holes x 34 holes
Cut 1

Poinettia Petals
21 holes x 21 holes
Cut 2

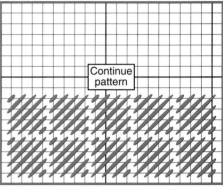

Holder Bottom
21 holes x 17 holes
Cut 1

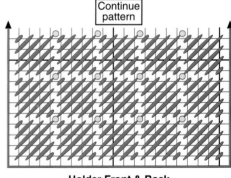

Holder Front & Back
21 holes x 45 holes
Cut 2

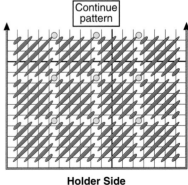

Holder Side
17 holes x 45 holes
Cut 2

COLOR KEY	
Worsted Weight Yarn	**Yards**
☐ Yellow	1
▨ Gold	2
▨ Green	2
■ Red	6
☐ White	4
■ Royal	50
✐ Black Straight Stitch	1
○ Light blue French Knot	7
● Gold French Knot	

Keepsake Christmas Frame

Design by Angie Arickx

A perfect frame for a perfect moment

1 Cut frame front from regular plastic canvas according to graph. Cut a 61-hole x 73-hole piece from stiff plastic canvas for frame back, cutting a 41-hole x 2-hole horizontal slit 10 holes from top and 10 holes from each side.

2 Stitch front only following graph. Overcast photo opening with holly. Back will remain unstitched.

3 Center and sew sawtooth hanger to top of frame back with white sewing thread. Whip-stitch front to back with red. ●

Beginner
Skill Level

Capture a special family moment on Christmas eve and display it in this sparkling frame throughout the holiday season.

Materials

- ☐ 1 sheet 7-count plastic canvas
- ☐ 1 sheet Darice Ultra Stiff 7-count plastic canvas
- ☐ Uniek Needloft plastic canvas yarn as listed in color key
- ☐ ⅛"-wide Plastic Canvas 7 Metallic Needlepoint Yarn by Rainbow Gallery as listed in color key
- ☐ #16 tapestry needle
- ☐ White sewing thread
- ☐ Sawtooth hanger

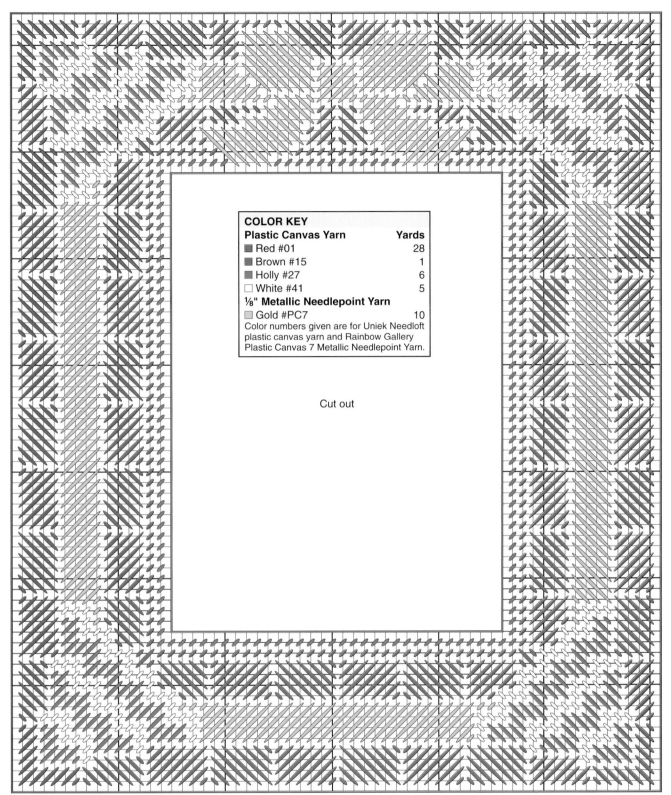

COLOR KEY

Plastic Canvas Yarn	Yards
■ Red #01	28
■ Brown #15	1
■ Holly #27	6
☐ White #41	5
⅛" Metallic Needlepoint Yarn	
☐ Gold #PC7	10

Color numbers given are for Uniek Needloft plastic canvas yarn and Rainbow Gallery Plastic Canvas 7 Metallic Needlepoint Yarn.

Cut out

Keepsake Christmas Frame Front
61 holes x 73 holes
Cut 1 from regular

Poinsettia Napkin Ring

Design by Judi Kauffman

A quick gift for a hostess

Beginner
Skill Level

You'll want to stitch a dozen of these enchanting napkin rings for Christmas dinner. A set of four makes a great gift, too!

Size

1³⁄₁₆" W x 1¾" diameter

Instructions

1 Cut plastic canvas according to graph.

2 Stitch as shown using 6 strands of embroidery floss or single strand of medium (#16) braid.

3 Using star green medium (#16) braid, Whipstitch short ends together. Using pearl ¹⁄₁₆" ribbon, Overcast remaining edges.

4 Glue ribbon flower to front of ring where indicated. Allow to dry thoroughly. ●

COLOR KEY

6-Strand Embroidery Floss	Yards
☐ White #1	3
■ Crimson red #46	3
Medium (#16) Braid	
■ Green #008	2½
☐ Flame #203	½
☐ Star green #9194	2
¹⁄₁₆" Ribbon	
⟋ Pearl #032 Overcasting	1¼
● Attach ribbon flower	
Color numbers given are for Anchor 6-strand embroidery floss and Kreinik Medium (#16) Braid and ¹⁄₁₆" Ribbon.	

Materials

- ☐ Small amount 14-count plastic canvas
- ☐ 6-strand embroidery floss* as listed in color key
- ☐ Medium (#16) metallic braid as listed in color key
- ☐ ¹⁄₁₆" metallic ribbon as listed in color key
- ☐ 1"-wide red, white or green ribbon flower with pearl center
- ☐ Tacky craft glue

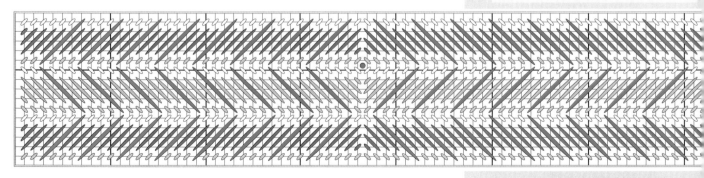

75 Merry Christmas Projects in Plastic Canvas

Poinsettia Napkin Ring
73 holes x 16 holes
Cut 1

A Beary Merry Christmas

Cuddly teddy bears bring comfort and cheer to each of us whether we're young, or simply young at heart. This collection of festive projects will add a warm feel to your Christmas.

Sled Ride Centerpiece

Design by Celia Lange Designs

Two adorable bears bring holiday cheer

A Beary Merry Christmas

Intermediate
Skill Level

Add warmth to your holiday table with this charming centerpiece! These two furry bears bring armloads of gifts and good cheer!

Materials

- ☐ 3 sheets Darice Ultra Stiff 7-count plastic canvas
- ☐ Chenille Sensations acrylic yarn from Lion Brand Yarn Co. as listed in color key
- ☐ Coats & Clark Red Heart Classic worsted weight yarn Art. E267 as listed in color key
- ☐ #16 tapestry needle
- ☐ Packing peanuts
- ☐ ½" white pompom
- ☐ ¼" white pompom
- ☐ ⅜" flat black shank button
- ☐ ¼" flat black shank button
- ☐ 2 (10mm) movable eyes
- ☐ 2 (8mm) movable eyes
- ☐ 8" artificial Christmas tree
- ☐ 3" holly candle ring
- ☐ 12" ⅜"-wide red satin ribbon
- ☐ 3 (1") decorated gift boxes
- ☐ Low-temperature glue gun

Cutting & Stitching

1. Cut plastic canvas according to graphs (pages 59–61).

2. Stitch pieces following graphs, reversing one sled runner before stitching. Backstitch mouths on bear heads with black.

3. Overcast sled runners, sled top, hearts, hatbands and all bear pieces with adjacent colors.

4. Using paddy green, Whipstitch support box long sides to support box short sides, then Whipstitch sides to support box bottom. Overcast top edges.

Assembly

1. Glue runners to support box long sides, placing box sides between arrows on sled runners. Fill support box with packing peanuts.

2. Using photo as a guide through step 9, center and glue sled top over support box and runners. Center and glue one heart to each runner.

3. Glue wrong side of hatbands to fronts and right side of hatbands to backs of corresponding teddy bear heads. Glue large pompom to tip of large bear hat and small pompom to tip of small bear hat.

4. For noses, glue large button to large bear head and small button to small bear head. Glue large movable eyes to large bear head and small movable eyes to small bear head.

COLOR KEY	
Chenille Acrylic Yarn	**Yards**
☐ White #100	8
■ Garnet #113	3
■ Mocha #125	27
■ Forest green #131	3
■ Brick #134	25
Worsted Weight Yarn	
■ Cherry red #912	26
■ Paddy green #686	43
✎ Black #12 Backstitch	1
Color numbers given are for Lion Brand Chenille Sensations acrylic yarn and Red Heart Classic worsted weight yarn Art. E267.	

5. Following Fig. 1 through step 6, glue bear bodies together, then glue heads to corresponding bodies. Glue tail to small bear.

Fig. 1

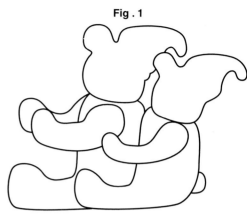

6. Glue one corresponding arm to each side of large bear. Glue upper arm only of one small bear arm to front of small bear. Glue remaining arm to backside of bears, placing shoulder at top edge of small bear body and hand over top edge of large bear body. *Note: Right side of arms are glued to backsides of bears.*

7. Center and glue bears to sled top. Bend branches of 8" tree so tree will lie flat against bears and sled. Glue in place, allowing branches to stick out.

8. Glue one gift package between hands of large bear. Glue remaining gift packages to sled behind large bear's leg.

9. For wreath, attach ribbon to candle ring and tie in a bow. Place wreath over arm on front of small bear; glue in place. ●

Sled Runner Heart
7 holes x 7 holes
Cut 2

Small Bear Tail
5 holes x 5 holes
Cut 1

Sled Ride Centerpiece

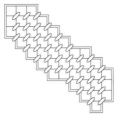

Small Bear Headband
10 holes x 10 holes
Cut 2

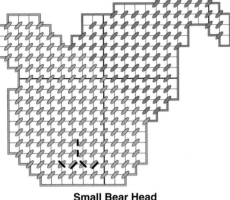

Small Bear Head
22 holes x 18 holes
Cut 1

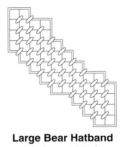

Small Bear Arm
20 holes x 9 holes
Cut 2

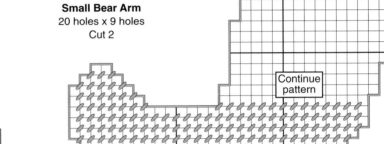

Continue pattern

Small Bear Body
30 holes x 25 holes
Cut 1

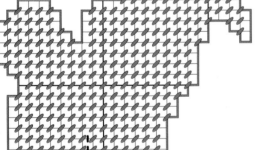

Large Bear Head
24 holes x 20 holes
Cut 1

Large Bear Hatband
10 holes x 10 holes
Cut 2

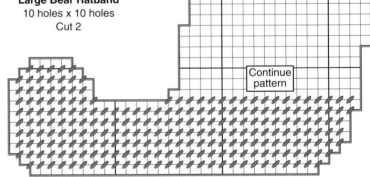

Continue pattern

Large Bear Body
34 holes x 29 holes
Cut 1

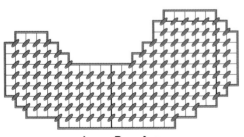

Large Bear Arm
22 holes x 11 holes
Cut 2

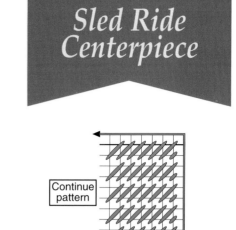
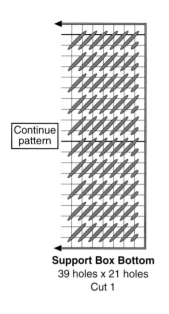

Continue pattern

Support Box Bottom
39 holes x 21 holes
Cut 1

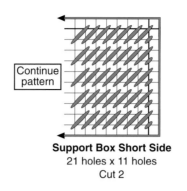

Continue pattern

Support Box Short Side
21 holes x 11 holes
Cut 2

Continue pattern

Support Box Long Side
39 holes x 11 holes
Cut 2

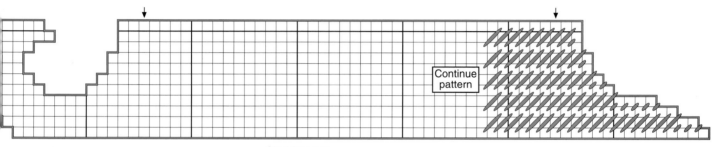

Continue pattern

Sled Runner
69 holes x 11 holes
Cut 2, reverse 1

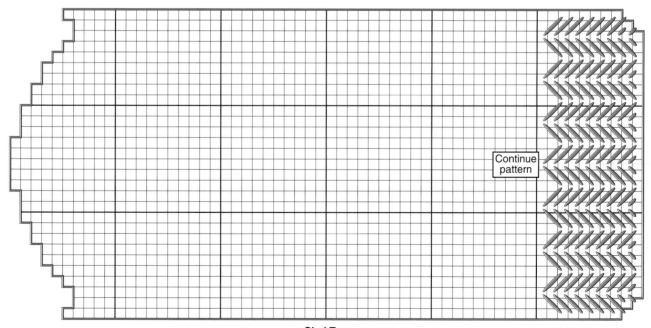

Continue pattern

Sled Top
60 holes x 29 holes
Cut 1

Beary Christmas Bag

Design by Michele Wilcox

Delight a hostess with two gifts in one

Instructions

1 Cut plastic canvas according to graphs (pages 62 and 63).

2 Stitch pieces following graphs, working Backstitches and French Knots with pearl cotton when background stitching is completed.

Beginner
Skill Level

Give two gifts in one with this adorable gift bag. It's just the right size for tucking a small hostess gift or party gift inside.

Materials

- ☐ 2 sheets 7-count plastic canvas
- ☐ Uniek Needloft plastic canvas yarn as listed in color key
- ☐ #5 pearl cotton as listed in color key
- ☐ #16 tapestry needle
- ☐ 2 (⁷⁄₁₆") yellow buttons
- ☐ Hot-glue gun

Continue pattern

Bag Handle
5 holes x 69 holes
Cut 1

Bag Front
33 holes x 53 holes
Cut 1

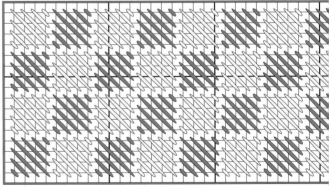

Bag Bottom
33 holes x 17 holes
Cut 1

3 With green pearl cotton, sew buttons to bear where indicated on bag front graph.

4 Using holly throughout, Overcast handle and top edges of front, back and sides. Whipstitch front and back to sides, then Whipstitch front, back and sides to bottom.

5 Center and glue handle ends inside bag front and back. ●

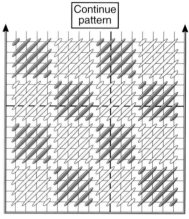

Continue pattern

Bag Side
17 holes x 53 holes
Cut 2

COLOR KEY

Plastic Canvas Yarn	Yards
■ Christmas red #02	5
■ Holly #27	30
□ Eggshell #39	48
□ Beige #40	1
■ Camel #43	8

Uncoded area on bag front is
eggshell #39 Continental Stitches

#5 Pearl Cotton

╱ Green Backstitch	2
╱ Black Backstitch	1
● Green French Knot	
● Black French Knot	
● Attach button	

Color numbers given are for Uniek Needloft plastic
canvas yarn.

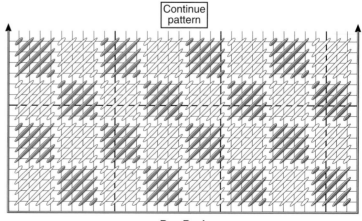

Continue pattern

Bag Back
33 holes x 53 holes
Cut 1

Peek-a-Boo Bear Stocking

Design by Angie Arickx

This cutie wants to play peek-a-boo

Instructions

1 Cut plastic canvas according to graphs (pages 64, 65 and 67).

2 Stitch pieces following graphs, working Backstitches on muzzle when background stitching is completed.

3 Overcast bow, paws and muzzle with adjacent colors. Overcast bear's head on stocking with gold and remaining edges with white.

4 Using photo as a guide, glue muzzle, paws and bow to stocking.

5 Hang as desired. ●

COLOR KEY	
Plastic Canvas Yarn	**Yards**
■ Christmas red #02	24
■ Brown #15	2
■ Gold #17	10
■ Christmas green #28	18
□ Beige #40	4
□ White #41	31
✎ Brown #15 Backstitch	
Color numbers given are for Uniek Needloft plastic canvas yarn.	

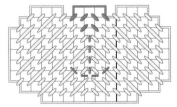

Peek-a-Boo Muzzle
15 holes x 9 holes
Cut 1

A Beary Merry Christmas

Beginner
Skill Level

Look who's peeking out from inside this Christmas stocking! Hang this festive decoration anywhere in your home to add holiday cheer and whimsy!

Materials

- ☐ ¾ artist-size sheet 7-count plastic canvas
- ☐ Uniek Needloft plastic canvas yarn as listed in color key
- ☐ #16 tapestry needle
- ☐ Hot-glue gun

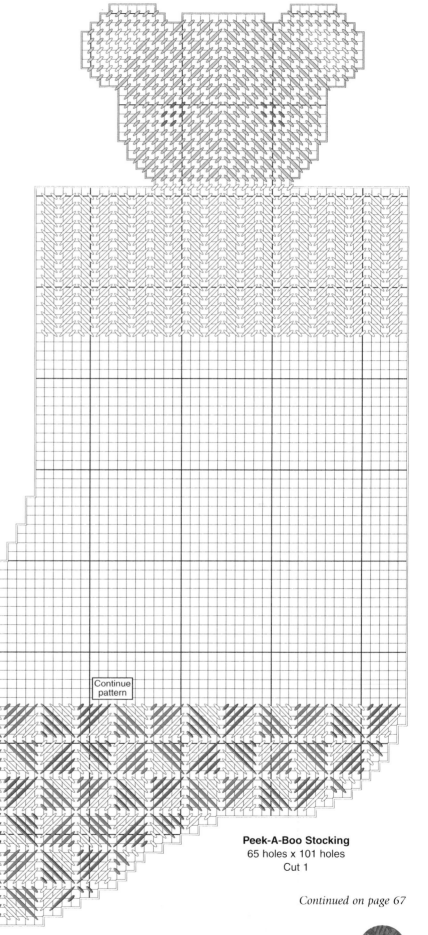

Continue pattern

Peek-A-Boo Stocking
65 holes x 101 holes
Cut 1

Continued on page 67

A Beary Merry Christmas 65

Little Angel Bear

Design by Mary T. Cosgrove

Stitch this diminutive darling tonight

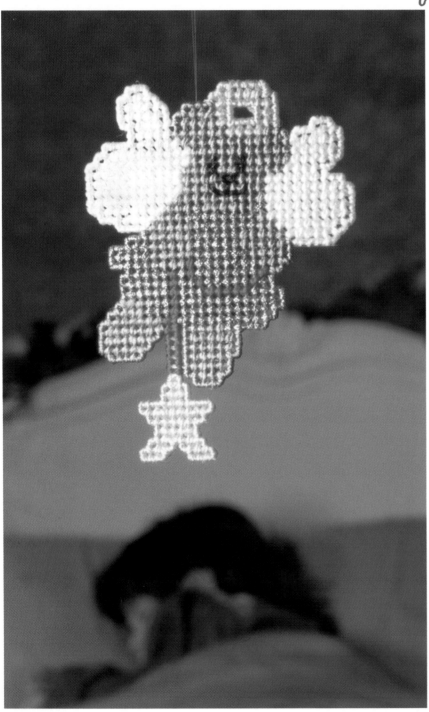

Beginner
Skill Level

Hang this darling angel ornament on your tree to delight the little ones in your family. Children can pretend she is their favorite stuffed animal's guardian angel!

Materials

- ☐ ⅓ sheet Uniek Quick-Count 7-count plastic canvas
- ☐ Uniek Needloft plastic canvas yarn as listed in color key
- ☐ Kreinik ⅛" Ribbon as listed in color key
- ☐ #16 tapestry needle
- ☐ Nylon thread

Use two strands when working with ⅛" ribbon.

Instructions

1 Cut plastic canvas according to graph.

2 Stitch piece following graph, working Backstitches when background stitching is completed. Overcast inside and outside edges following graph.

3 Thread desired length nylon thread through stitches on top backside just to the left of halo. Tie ends in a knot to form a loop for hanging. ●

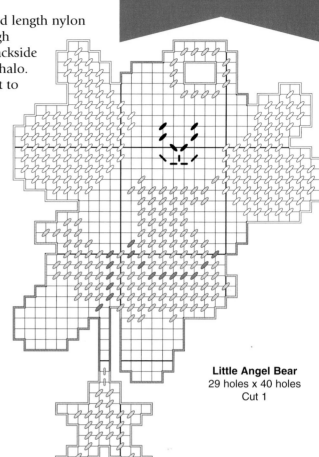

Little Angel Bear
29 holes x 40 holes
Cut 1

COLOR KEY

Plastic Canvas Yarn	Yards
■ Black #00	1
■ Red #01	1
□ White #41	4
□ Yellow #57	2
Uncoded areas are camel #43 Continental Stitches	4
⁄ Camel #43 Overcasting	
⁄ Black #00 Backstitch	
⁄ Yellow #57 Backstitch	
⅛" Ribbon	
□ Sky blue #014HL	5

Color numbers given are for Uniek Needloft plastic canvas yarn and Kreinik ⅛" Ribbon.

Peek-a-Boo Stocking

Continued from page 65

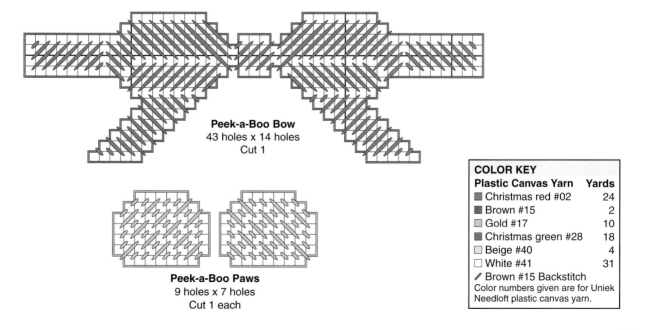

Peek-a-Boo Bow
43 holes x 14 holes
Cut 1

Peek-a-Boo Paws
9 holes x 7 holes
Cut 1 each

COLOR KEY

Plastic Canvas Yarn	Yards
■ Christmas red #02	24
■ Brown #15	2
□ Gold #17	10
■ Christmas green #28	18
□ Beige #40	4
□ White #41	31
⁄ Brown #15 Backstitch	

Color numbers given are for Uniek Needloft plastic canvas yarn.

Angelic Bear

Design by Joan Green

A special gift for a little girl

Cutting & Stitching

1 Cut plastic canvas according to graphs (pages 70 and 71).

2 Stitch pieces following graphs, working uncoded background on sign with natural Continental Stitches and uncoded area on bear's dress with pale sea green Continental Stitches.

3 Complete the lettering on sign with 4-ply dark lagoon Backstitches. Backstitch mouth on muzzle with 4 plies warm brown. Work French Knots on letters and at top of head with 4 plies medium orchid.

4 Backstitch outlining on dress with 2 plies medium orchid and holly leaves on dress with 2 plies dark lagoon. Work French Knots on dress with 2 plies medium orchid and on wings with 2 plies pale orchid.

5 Overcast star with sunshine, sign with light orchid and muzzle with honey. Overcast bear with pale orchid, light orchid and honey following graph.

Assembly

1 Using photo as a guide throughout assembly, with sewing needle and gold thread, attach gold star button to center of stitched star.

2 Using sunshine yarn throughout, tack stitched star to bear front below hands using sunshine yarn. Work Long Stitches from holes indicated with blue dots at top of star to holes indicated with blue dots at bottom of paws.

3 Tack muzzle in place over unstitched portion of face at muzzle corners.

4 Cut a 6" length of ribbon and tie in a bow; trim ends as desired. Center and glue to dress collar.

5 Cut remaining ribbon into two 12" lengths. For hanging ribbon on left side, knot one end of one length, then thread other end through stitches on backside of sign just above hole indicated for attaching hanging ribbon, pulling until knot is against sign.

6 Thread ribbon from back to front through hole indicated on left wing of bear, then thread from front to back through hole on sign. Weave end through stitching on backside, allowing 3" between the two pieces; knot ribbon. Secure knots with small amount of glue.

7 Repeat steps 5 and 6 with remaining ribbon on right side of sign.

8 Wrap 20-gauge wire around pencil. Remove pencil and loosen coils. Bend wire, then center hanger and glue ends to top backside of sign. ●

Beginner
Skill Level

Delight your little girl by stitching this beautiful Christmas bear to hang on her bedroom door or wall. She'll look forward to hanging it year after year!

Materials

- ☐ 1½ sheets 7-count plastic canvas
- ☐ Spinrite Bernat Berella "4" worsted weight yarn as listed in color key
- ☐ #16 tapestry needle
- ☐ Gold star button #86016 by Mill Hill Products from Gay Bowles Sales Inc.
- ☐ Sewing needle and gold thread
- ☐ 30" ⅛"-wide rose satin ribbon
- ☐ 18" 20-gauge green cloth-covered wire
- ☐ Pencil
- ☐ Hot-glue gun

Angelic Bear
51 holes x 67 holes
Cut 1

COLOR KEY

Worsted Weight Yarn	Yards
☐ Sunshine #8701	3
☐ Pale orchid #8768	12
☐ Light orchid #8769	14
☐ Medium orchid #8770	9
☐ Honey #8795	16
☐ Warm brown #8797	1
☐ Dark lagoon #8822	10
☐ Natural #8940	26
Uncoded areas on bear's dress are pale sea green #8879 Continental Stitches	6
Uncoded area on sign is natural #8940 Continental Stitches	
╱ Medium orchid #8770 Backstitch	
╱ Dark lagoon #8822 Backstitch	
╱ Warm brown #8797 Backstitch	
○ Pale orchid #8768 French Knot	
● Medium orchid #8770 French Knot	
● Attach hanging ribbon	

Color numbers given are for Spinrite Bernat Berella "4" worsted weight yarn.

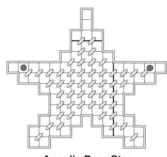

Angelic Bear Muzzle
7 holes x 7 holes
Cut 1

Angelic Bear Star
15 holes x 13 holes
Cut 1

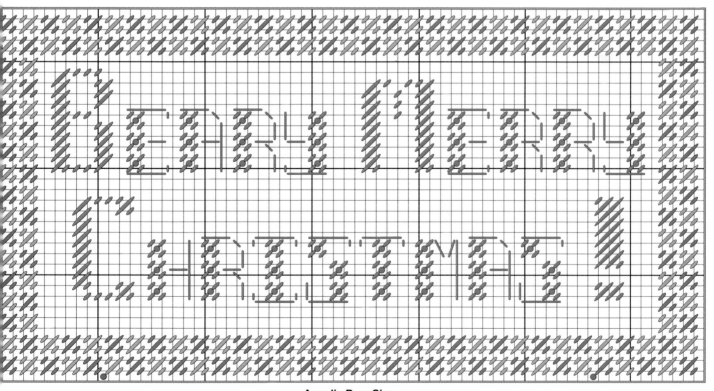

Angelic Bear Sign
67 holes x 35 holes
Cut 1

"Waiting for Santa" Christmas Card Box

Design by Celia Lange Designs

A festive holder for Christmas cards

Instructions

1 Cut plastic canvas according to graphs (pages 72 and 74).

2 Stitch pieces following graphs, reversing one bench outer side and one bench inner side before stitching. Stitch box back, bench inner sides and seat back with cornmeal Continental Stitches only.

3 When background stitching is completed, work dark sage Straight Stitches on seat front and new berry French Knots on box front and sides, bench outer sides and seat front.

4 Using cornmeal through step 6, Overcast top edges of box front, back and sides. Whipstitch front and back to sides, then Whipstitch front, back and sides to bottom.

5 With wrong sides facing and matching edges, Whipstitch one bench inner side and one bench outer side together. Repeat with remaining bench sides.

6 Whipstitch bench seat front and back to bench seat ends, then Whipstitch seat front, back and ends to seat top and bottom.

7 Using photo as a guide through step 9, glue bench seat to bench sides, then glue bench to box front, making sure bottom edges are even.

8 Wrap 3½" bear in quilt, putting flocked bear in 3½" bear's lap; glue to left side of seat top, securing quilt under seat bottom.

9 Fold white paper in half. With black marker, print "For Santa" on bottom half. Glue platter of goodies, cup or mug and "For Santa" note to seat top. ●

Intermediate
Skill Level

This little cutie will watch over your Christmas cards while he waits up for Santa—if he doesn't fall asleep first.

Materials

☐ 2 sheets Darice Ultra Stiff 7-count plastic canvas

☐ Coats & Clark Red Heart Classic worsted weight yarn Art. E267 as listed in color key

☐ #16 tapestry needle

☐ 3½" light tan jointed bear

☐ 1" brown flocked sitting bear

☐ 7" square doll quilt

☐ Miniature platter of treats

☐ Miniature cup and saucer or mug

☐ 1⅛" square white paper

☐ Black fine-point marker

☐ Low-temperature glue gun

Box Seat End
13 holes x 3 holes
Cut 2

COLOR KEY

Worsted Weight Yarn	Yards
☐ Cornmeal #220	108
■ Dark sage #633	9
╱ Dark sage #633 Straight Stitch	
● New berry #760 French Knot	3

Color numbers given are for Red Heart Classic worsted weight yarn Art. E267.

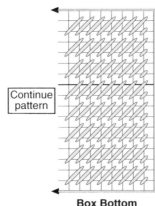

Continue pattern

Box Bottom
49 holes x 17 holes
Cut 1

"Waiting for Santa" Christmas Card Box

Bench Seat Front & Back
43 holes x 3 holes
Cut 2
Stitch embroidery on
front only

COLOR KEY

Worsted Weight Yarn	Yards
☐ Cornmeal #220	108
■ Dark sage #633	9
╱ Dark sage #633 Straight Stitch	
● New berry #760 French Knot	3

Color numbers given are for Red Heart Classic
worsted weight yarn Art. E267.

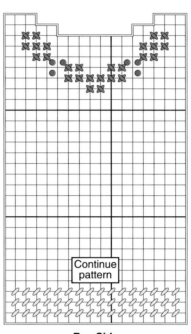

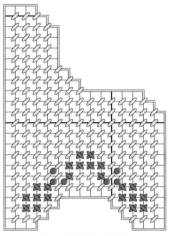

Bench Outer Side
15 holes x 21 holes
Cut 2, reverse 1

Bench Inner Side
15 holes x 21 holes
Cut 2, reverse 1
Stitch with Continental
Stitches only

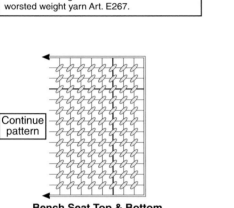

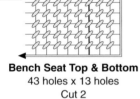

Continue
pattern

Bench Seat Top & Bottom
43 holes x 13 holes
Cut 2

Continue
pattern

Box Side
17 holes x 29 holes
Cut 2

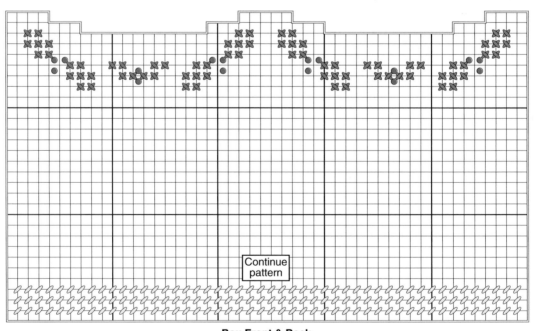

Continue
pattern

Box Front & Back
49 holes x 29 holes
Cut 2
Stitch back with
Continental Stitches only

75 Merry Christmas Projects in Plastic Canvas

Teddy Bear Pocket Pals

Designs by Joan Green

Quick to stitch and bursting with cheer

Instructions

1 Cut plastic canvas according to graphs (page 76).

2 Stitch pieces following graphs. Do not stitch lower portion of bears. When background stitching is completed work French Knots with 4 plies black and Backstitches with 2 plies black.

3 Overcast bears around sides and top from dot to dot following graphs. Overcast top edge of boy bear pocket front with honey. Overcast top edge of girl bear pocket front with dark lagoon.

4 Matching edges, place wrong side of pocket fronts on right side of unstitched portion of corresponding bears. Whipstitch together around sides and bottom following graphs.

5 Cut ribbon in half. Tie each half in a bow. Glue one bow to each bear at neckline. Trim ends as desired.

6 Insert tiny candy cane, rolled-up money or small item as desired in pockets. ●

Beginner

Skill Level

Tuck a little Christmas cheer into either of these diminutive bears! They're a perfect holiday gift for the young and young at heart!

Materials

- ☐ ½ sheet 7-count plastic canvas
- ☐ Spinrite Bernat Berella "4" worsted weight yarn as listed in color key
- ☐ #16 tapestry needle
- ☐ 16" ⅛"-wide red satin ribbon
- ☐ Hot-glue gun

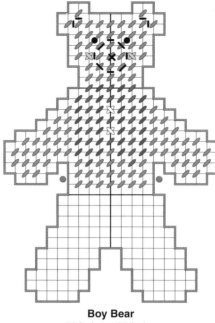

Boy Bear
20 holes x 28 holes
Cut 1

Girl Bear
20 holes x 28 holes
Cut 1

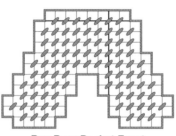

Boy Bear Pocket Front
16 holes x 11 holes
Cut 1

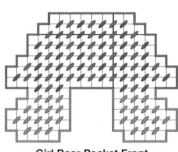

Girl Bear Pocket Front
16 holes x 12 holes
Cut 1

COLOR KEY
BOY BEAR

Worsted Weight Yarn	Yards
■ Honey #8795	7
■ Dark lagoon #8822	1
■ Rose #8921	½
■ Scarlet #8933	1
☐ White #8942	½
■ Black #8994	½
╱ Black #8994 Backstitch	
● Black #8994 French Knot	

Color numbers given are for Spinrite Bernat Berella "4" worsted weight yarn.

COLOR KEY
GIRL BEAR

Worsted Weight Yarn	Yards
■ Honey #8795	4
■ Dark lagoon #8822	3
■ Rose #8921	½
■ Scarlet #8933	2
☐ White #8942	1
■ Black #8994	½
╱ Black #8994 Backstitch	
● Black #8994 French Knot	

Color numbers given are for Spinrite Bernat Berella "4" worsted weight yarn.

Teddy in a Wagon

Design by Ruby Thacker

Santa's helper is loaded with gifts

Intermediate
Skill Level

Add a festive touch to any small corner in your home with this charming accent piece. This sweet bear is ready to decorate his tree and place a stack of colorful gifts underneath it!

Materials

- ☐ ½ sheet red 7-count plastic canvas
- ☐ ¼ sheet black 7-count plastic canvas
- ☐ Uniek Needloft plastic canvas yarn as listed in color key
- ☐ #16 tapestry needle
- ☐ Safety pins
- ☐ 4 (1") toy wooden wheels
- ☐ 2 (3½") lengths ¼"-diameter wooden dowels
- ☐ Black and red acrylic paint
- ☐ Paintbrush
- ☐ 3½" light tan jointed bear
- ☐ 9" ⅜"-wide red ribbon
- ☐ 3 miniature gift boxes in assorted sizes
- ☐ 5mm x 8mm plastic light bulbs #2420-11 in assorted colors from Darice Inc.
- ☐ Miniature Christmas tree
- ☐ Wood glue
- ☐ Hot-glue gun

Instructions

1 Cut wagon bottom, floor and side from red plastic canvas; cut undercarriage and handle from black plastic canvas according to graphs (page 78). Wagon bottom, handle and undercarriage will remain unstitched.

2 Stitch wagon floor and side following graphs, overlapping five holes on short ends of side before stitching.

3 With black, Whipstitch end on handle to tongue end of undercarriage, then Overcast remaining inner and outer edges of handle and edges indicated from blue dot to blue dot on undercarriage.

4 Place undercarriage on top of wagon bottom and insert tabs of undercarriage through slots on bottom. Place wrong side of wagon floor on top of undercarriage, matching floor edges with wagon bottom edges. This forms the wagon base.

5 Place bottom edge of wagon side on outside edges of wagon base. Secure all layers with safety pins to prevent slipping. With red, Whipstitch side to base through all layers, removing safety pins as you go. Overcast top edge

A Beary Merry Christmas

of wagon side with red Braided Cross Stitch (Fig. 1).

6 Bend tabs on undercarriage down; insert dowels through holes on tabs. Slip wheels on ends of dowels; attach with wood glue to secure.

7 Using photo as a guide through step 8, paint center of wheels red and rims black. Allow to dry.

8 Tie ribbon in a bow around teddy bear's neck. Trim ends as desired. Using hot glue throughout, seat bear in wagon; glue in place. Glue tree in one arm. Drape several lights over other shoulder and glue in place. Glue gift packages in wagon. ●

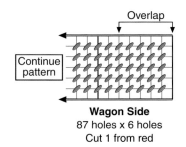

COLOR KEY	
Plastic Canvas Yarn	**Yards**
■ Red #01	18
✓ Black #00 Overcasting and Whipstitching	1
Color numbers given are for Uniek Needloft plastic canvas yarn.	

Fig. 1
Braided Cross Stitch

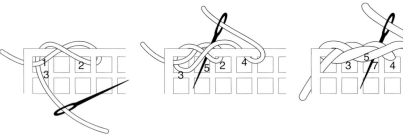

To begin, bring needle from back to front at 1, over edge and from back to front at 2, over edge and from back to front and under yarn at 3, pulling yarn tight.

Pulling yarn tight with each stitch, continue by bringing needle over edge and from back to front at 4, over edge and from back to front at 5, etc.

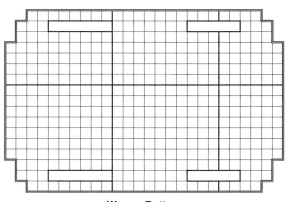

Overlap

Continue pattern

Wagon Side
87 holes x 6 holes
Cut 1 from red

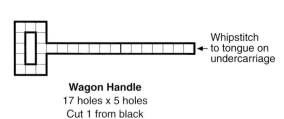

Whipstitch to tongue on undercarriage →

Wagon Handle
17 holes x 5 holes
Cut 1 from black
Do not stitch

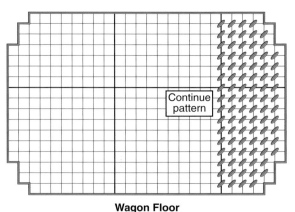

Wagon Bottom
26 holes x 17 holes
Cut 1 from red
Do not stitch

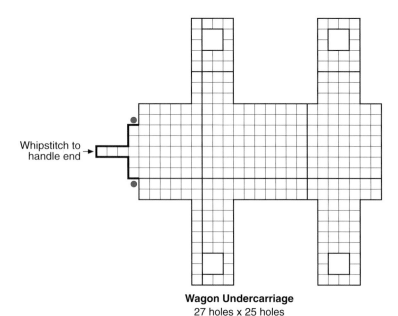

Whipstitch to handle end →

Wagon Undercarriage
27 holes x 25 holes
Cut 1 from black
Do not stitch

Continue pattern

Wagon Floor
26 holes x 17 holes
Cut 1 from red

Christmas in the Country

If you enjoy the warmth of a country decor, then you'll find many handy and decorative home accessories in this chapter to add to your holiday celebration.

Winter Spruce
Table Set

Designs by Angie Arickx

An attractive quilt-style table set

75 Merry Christmas Projects in Plastic Canvas

Christmas in the Country

Beginner
Skill Level

Stitch this handsome pine tree place mat, napkin ring and coaster set to use before, during and after the holidays.

Materials

- ☐ 1¼ (12" x 18") sheets Darice Super Soft 7-count plastic canvas
- ☐ Uniek Needloft plastic canvas yarn as listed in color key
- ☐ #16 tapestry needle

Instructions

1 Cut plastic canvas according to graphs (pages 81 and 84).

2 Stitch pieces following graphs, overlapping two opposite corners on napkin ring where indicated with blue dots when stitching.

3 Overcast all edges with white. ●

COLOR KEY	
Plastic Canvas Yarn	**Yards**
■ Red #01	57
■ Maple #13	10
■ Holly #27	48
☐ White #41	58
Color numbers given are for Uniek Needloft plastic canvas yarn.	

Graphs continued on page 84

Winter Spruce Place Mat
117 holes x 79 holes
Cut 1

Continue pattern

Gingerbread Plaque

Design by Celia Lange Designs

"Catch me if you can!"

Beginner
Skill Level

Everyone loves the aroma of fresh-from-the-oven gingerbread! With this charming wall plaque, you can add a delightful sight to the mouth-watering smells!

Materials

- ☐ 1 sheet Darice Ultra Stiff 7-count plastic canvas
- ☐ Coats & Clark Red Heart Super Saver worsted weight yarn Art. E301 as listed in color key
- ☐ Coats & Clark Red Heart Classic worsted weight yarn Art. E267 as listed in color key
- ☐ #16 tapestry needle
- ☐ ⅜" red heart button
- ☐ 6½" rolling pin
- ☐ Low-temperature glue gun

Cutting & Stitching

1 Cut plastic canvas according to graphs (pages 83 and 84).

2 Stitch pieces following graphs. When background stitching is completed, work black Backstitches for letters on plaque, then add cardinal French Knots.

3 For border on plaque, add cardinal Running Stitches, working Backstitches at corners; add dark sage and warm brown French Knots.

4 Work black Backstitches and French Knots on gingerbread man and black Backstitches on heart.

5 Using warm brown through out, Overcast plaque edges. For gingerbread man, Whipstitch bottom edge of upper body to top edge of lower body; Overcast remaining edges. Backstitch cuffs on arms and legs with Aran, wrapping stitches around edges.

6 Overcast heart edges with black.

Assembly

1 Cut 1-yard lengths each of warm brown, dark sage and claret yarn. Place lengths together and knot each end securely. Twist knots in opposite directions, until yarn is tightly twisted. Fold in half, bringing knotted ends together; allow halves to twist around each other. Tie knotted ends together.

2 Using photo as a guide through step 5, glue knotted end in one upper back corner of plaque and folded end in remaining upper back corner. Tie a loop in center of twisted cord.

3 For rolling pin swing, follow instructions for step 1 to make two more twisted cords using 18" lengths for each cord.

4 Insert one rolling pin handle through folded end of each cord. Glue knotted ends of cords to back of plaque, making sure lengths are even. If desired, using a small amount of glue, secure yarn to rolling pin handles.

5 Glue or sew heart button to gingerbread man, then glue lower body of gingerbread man to rolling pin; glue hand to cord. ●

COLOR KEY

Worsted Weight Yarn	Yards
☐ Aran #313	25
☐ Buff #334	24
☐ Warm brown #336	14
☐ Rose pink #372	1
☐ Light sage #631	1
☐ Dark sage #633	5
☐ Claret #762	3
✦ Black #312 Backstitch and Overcasting	5
✦ Aran #313 Backstitch	
✦ Cardinal #917 Backstitch and Running Stitch	4
● Black #310 French Knot	
● Warm brown #336 French Knot	
● Dark sage #633 French Knot	
● Cardinal #917 French Knot	

Color numbers given are for Red Heart Super Saver worsted weight yarn Art. E301 and Red Heart Classic worsted weight yarn Art. E267.

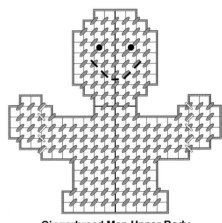

Gingerbread Man Upper Body
20 holes x 19 holes
Cut 1

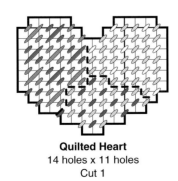

Quilted Heart
14 holes x 11 holes
Cut 1

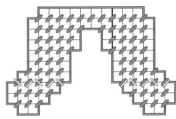

Gingerbread Man Lower Body
16 holes x 10 holes
Cut 1

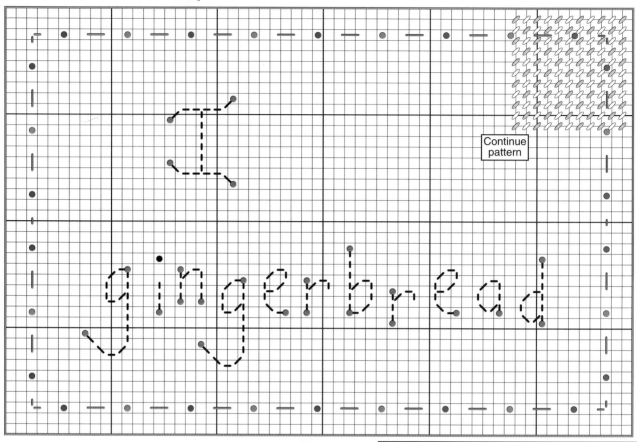

Plaque
59 holes x 40 holes
Cut 1

Winter Spruce Table Set

Continued from page 81

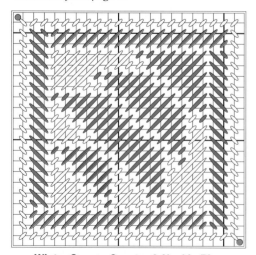

Winter Spruce Coaster & Napkin Ring
22 holes x 22 holes
Cut 1 for coaster
Cut 1 for napkin ring

COLOR KEY

Worsted Weight Yarn	Yards
☐ Aran #313	25
▦ Buff #334	24
▨ Warm brown #336	14
▨ Rose pink #372	1
☐ Light sage #631	1
■ Dark sage #633	5
■ Claret #762	3
✦ Black #312 Backstitch and Overcasting	5
✧ Aran #313 Backstitch	
✦ Cardinal #917 Backstitch and Running Stitch	4
● Black #310 French Knot	
● Warm brown #336 French Knot	
● Dark sage #633 French Knot	
● Cardinal #917 French Knot	

Color numbers given are for Red Heart Super Saver worsted weight yarn Art. E301 and Red Heart Classic worsted weight yarn Art. E267.

COLOR KEY

Plastic Canvas Yarn	Yards
■ Red #01	57
■ Maple #13	10
■ Holly #27	48
☐ White #41	58

Color numbers given are for Uniek Needloft plastic canvas yarn.

A perfect last-minute hostess gift

Beginner

Skill Level

This delightful hostess gift is sure to be appreciated, and is very quick to stitch and assemble!

Materials

- ☐ Small amount 7-count plastic canvas
- ☐ Uniek Needloft plastic canvas yarn as listed in color key
- ☐ Kreinik Very Fine (#4) Braid as listed in color key
- ☐ DMC #3 pearl cotton as listed in color key
- ☐ DMC #5 pearl cotton as listed in color key
- ☐ #16 tapestry needle
- ☐ 6½" basket
- ☐ Dark green twisted paper ribbon
- ☐ Natural raffia
- ☐ Excelsior
- ☐ Gift, pinecones or basket filler as desired
- ☐ Long needle and carpet thread (optional)
- ☐ Thick white glue

Instructions

1 Cut plastic canvas according to graph (page 87).

2 Stitch house following graph, working uncoded area with violet Continental Stitches. Overcast with adjacent colors, excluding smoke edges, which will remain unstitched.

3 Work pearl braid Cross Stitches over snow eggshell stitches where indicated on graph.

4 Backstitch smoke with eggshell and wreath with forest. Add ecru #3 pearl cotton Backstitches and Straight Stitches to door and windows. Add black #5 pearl cotton Backstitches and Straight Stitches to door and windows; work a double Straight Stitch for doorknob.

5 Use photo as a guide through out assembly. For bow streamer, cut a 14" length of dark green twisted

Continued on page 87

Santa Mouse Coasters

Design by Michele Wilcox

Stitch a complete set of fun coasters

75 Merry Christmas Projects in Plastic Canvas

Christmas in the Country

Beginner
Skill Level

This festive coasters set is as decorative as it is practical! Each mouse coaster is just the right size for placing under a mug of hot chocolate!

Materials

- □ 1 sheet 7-count plastic canvas
- □ Uniek Needloft plastic canvas yarn as listed in color key
- □ DMC #3 pearl cotton as listed in color key
- □ #16 tapestry needle
- □ Small basket to hold 4 coasters

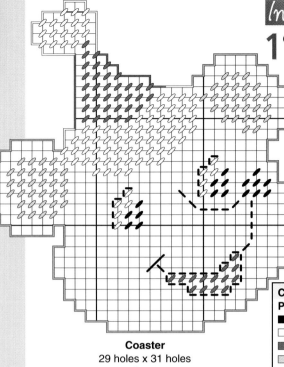

Coaster
29 holes x 31 holes
Cut 4

Instructions

1 Cut four coasters from plastic canvas according to graph.

2 Stitch coasters following graph, working uncoded areas with silver Continental Stitches.

3 Work Backstitches with black pearl cotton when background stitching is completed. Overcast following graph. ●

COLOR KEY

Plastic Canvas Yarn	Yards
■ Black #00	2
□ White #41	8
■ Crimson #42	6
□ Coral #66	8
Uncoded area is silver #37 Continental Stitches	40
⁄ Silver #37 Overcasting	
#3 Pearl Cotton	
⁄ Black #310 Backstitch	5
Color numbers given are for Uniek Needloft plastic canvas yarn and DMC #3 pearl cotton.	

From Our House to Yours
Continued from page 85

paper ribbon. Cut an inverted "V" in both ends; center and glue to basket front, wrapping around sides and gluing ends to handles.

6 Form a 6" bow with natural raffia and twisted paper ribbon. Center and glue

bow to streamer on basket front. Glue stitched house over center of bow. If desired, reinforce assembly by tacking to basket with long needle and carpet thread.

7 Fill basket with excelsior and gift, pinecones or basket filler as desired. ●

COLOR KEY

Plastic Canvas Yarn	Yards
■ Black #00	2
■ Forest #29	2
□ Eggshell #39	4
▨ Camel #43	1
Uncoded area is violet #04 Continental Stitches	2
⁄ Violet #04 Overcasting	
⁄ Forest #29 Backstitch	
⁄ Eggshell #39 Backstitch	
Very Fine (#4) Braid	
⁄ Pearl #032 Cross Stitch	3
#3 Pearl Cotton	
⁄ Ecru Backstitch and Straight Stitch	2
#5 Pearl Cotton	
⁄ Black #310 Backstitch and Straight Stitch	2
Color numbers given are for Uniek Needloft plastic canvas yarn, Kreinik Very Fine (#4) Braid and DMC #3 pearl cotton and #5 pearl cotton.	

House
31 holes x 23 holes
Cut 1

Poinsettia Garland Basket

Design by Angie Arickx

Perfect poinsettias twine this basket

Instructions

1 Cut plastic canvas according to graphs.

2 Stitch pieces following graphs, leaving straw stitches in centers of poinsettia pieces unworked at this time. Work eggshell French Knots on garland sections when background stitching is completed.

3 Overcast garland sections with forest and petals on poinsettia pieces with crimson.

4 For each flower, place one poinsettia front on one poinsettia back so that petals on front are centered between petals on back. Work straw stitches in center, securing front to back.

5 Using photo as a guide, glue poinsettias to garland sections, forming a circle. With wire, attach one poinsettia under handle on each side of basket. Glue remaining six poinsettias to basket rim, sanding rim where attaching poinsettias so glue will adhere. ●

Filled with fresh-from-the-oven rolls or other baked goodies, this pretty basket is as pretty as it is practical!

Materials

- ☐ 1 sheet 7-count plastic canvas
- ☐ Uniek Needloft plastic canvas yarn as listed in color key
- ☐ #16 tapestry needle
- ☐ Small amount 24-gauge wire
- ☐ Wicker basket with 31"–32" circumference
- ☐ Sandpaper
- ☐ Hot-glue gun

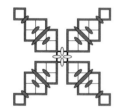

Poinsettia Front
9 holes x 9 holes
Cut 8

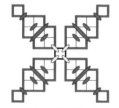

Poinsettia Back
9 holes x 9 holes
Cut 8

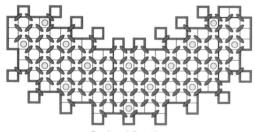

Garland Section
23 holes x 11 holes
Cut 8

COLOR KEY	
Plastic Canvas Yarn	**Yards**
☐ Straw #19	2
■ Forest #29	35
■ Crimson #42	20
○ Eggshell #39 French Knot	8
Color numbers given are for Uniek Needloft plastic canvas yarn.	

Merry Christmas Country Blocks

Design by Angie Arickx

Stitch a "Merry Christmas!" to all

1 Cut plastic canvas according to graphs (page 91).

2 Stitch front, back, sides and top following graphs, working uncoded areas with eggshell Continental Stitches. Bottom will remain unstitched.

3 Following graphs through step 4, Overcast inside edges indicated on front and back. On front, back, top and sides, Overcast edges of indents on outside edges as indicated.

4 Using Cross Stitches, Whipstitch front and back to top and bottom, then Whipstitch front, back, top and bottom to sides. ●

Christmas in the Country

Beginner
Skill Level

Wish all who visit your home during the holidays a merry Christmas with this eye-catching shelf accent adorned with hearts and holly!

Materials

- ☐ 1 sheet 7-count plastic canvas
- ☐ Uniek Needloft plastic canvas yarn as listed in color key
- ☐ #16 tapestry needle

COLOR KEY	
Plastic Canvas Yarn	**Yards**
■ Forest #29	43
■ Crimson #42	42
Uncoded areas are eggshell #39 Continental Stitches	36
Color numbers given are for Uniek Needloft plastic canvas yarn.	

Blocks Side
8 holes x 17 holes
Cut 2

Blocks Front & Back
80 holes x 17 holes
Cut 2

Blocks Top & Bottom
80 holes x 8 holes
Cut 2, stitch 1

Country Pine Stocking

Design by Mary T. Cosgrove

A stocking even men will like

Instructions

1 Cut one stocking from clear plastic canvas for stocking front and one from almond plastic canvas for stocking back according to graph (page 93). Stocking back will remain unstitched.

2 For stocking front, stitch cuff first, then bottom part following graph.

3 Cut an 8" length of burgundy yarn. Thread ends from back to front through holes indicated on stocking front with blue dots. Tie yarn in a bow; trim ends as desired.

4 Matching edges, place stocking front and back together. Using burgundy, Whipstitch together around sides and bottom; Overcast top edges.

5 For hanging loop, cut an 8" length of burgundy yarn. Thread through both layers from front to back where indicated on graph. Knot ends together on backside. ●

COLOR KEY	
Plastic Canvas Yarn	**Yards**
■ Burgundy #03	22
■ Forest #29	19
□ Eggshell #03	27
● Attach hanging loop	
Color numbers given are for Uniek Needloft plastic canvas yarn.	

Christmas in the Country

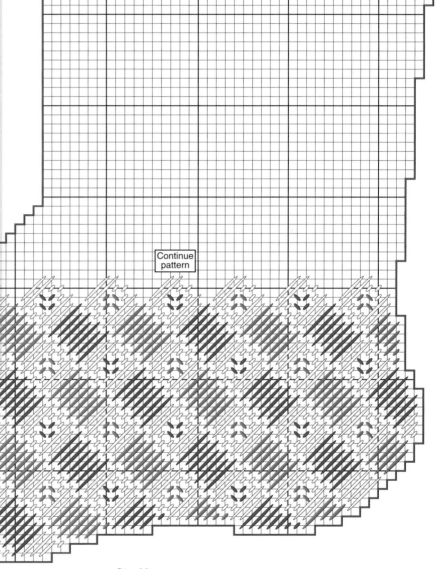

Beginner
Skill Level

Stitch this handsome stocking for your hard-to-please man of the house. With its rich Christmas colors and simple pine tree design, he'll enjoy hanging it year after year.

Materials

- ☐ 1 sheet Uniek Quick-Count clear 7-count plastic canvas
- ☐ 1 sheet Uniek Quick-Count almond 7-count plastic canvas
- ☐ Uniek Needloft plastic canvas yarn as listed in color key
- ☐ #16 tapestry needle

Continue pattern

Stocking
67 holes x 90 holes
Cut 1 from clear for front
Stitch as graphed
Cut 1 from almond for back
Do not stitch

Country Home Accents

Designs by Mary T. Cosgrove

Easy home accents in no time at all

House Napkin Ring

Instructions

1 Cut one house and one ring from plastic canvas according to graphs (page 96).

2 Stitch background on house following graph, working uncoded area with eggshell Continental Stitches.

3 When background stitching is completed, work Backstitches using 1 ply forest. Overcast with burgundy.

4 Overlap four holes on ring as indicated, then Overcast edges with eggshell, then work burgundy Running Stitches.

5 Using eggshell, securely fasten overlapped edges of ring to yarn on center backside of house.

Tree Napkin Ring

Instructions

1 Cut one tree and one ring from plastic canvas according to graphs (page 96).

2 Stitch tree following graph. Overcast with eggshell.

3 Overlap four holes on ring as indicated, then Overcast edges with eggshell, then work burgundy Running Stitches.

4 Using small paintbrush and butter cream paint, outline edges of heart-shaped beads. Allow to dry thoroughly.

5 When paint is dry, sew beads to front of stitched tree where indicated on graph with 2 plies deep antique mauve floss.

6 Using eggshell yarn, securely fasten overlapped edges of ring to yarn on center backside of tree.

Magnet

Instructions

1 Cut one magnet according to graph (page 96).

2 Stitch piece following graph, working uncoded area on house with eggshell Continental Stitches.

3 When background stitching is completed, work Backstitches using 1 ply forest. Overcast house edges with burgundy and tree edges with eggshell.

4 Glue magnetic strip to back of stitched piece. ●

Beginner
Skill Level

Each of these napkin rings takes less than an hour to stitch, and will add a hand-stitched, country look to your buffet table. Combine the two motifs for a handy refrigerator magnet.

Materials

House Napkin Ring
☐ Small amount 7-count plastic canvas
☐ Uniek Needloft plastic canvas yarn as listed in color key
☐ #16 tapestry needle

Tree Napkin Ring
☐ Small amount 7-count plastic canvas
☐ Uniek Needloft plastic canvas yarn as listed in color key
☐ #16 tapestry needle
☐ 3 (¼") Whimsy crystal red #7040 heart-shaped glass beads from Wichelt Imports

Continued on page 96

Country Home Accents

Materials

Continued from page 94

☐ 12" DMC 6-strand embroidery floss: deep antique
mauve #3802

☐ Ceramcoat acrylic paint by
Delta Technical Coatings
Inc.: butter cream #2523

☐ Small paintbrush

Magnet

☐ Small amount 7-count
plastic canvas

☐ Uniek Needloft plastic
canvas yarn as listed in
color key

☐ #16 tapestry needle

☐ 1½" length ½"-wide
magnetic strip

☐ Hot-glue gun

COLOR KEY
HOUSE NAPKIN RING

Plastic Canvas Yarn	Yards
■ Burgundy #03	1½
Uncoded area is eggshell #39 Continental Stitches	2
⁄ Eggshell #39 Overcasting	
⁄ Burgundy #03 Running Stitch	
⁄ Forest #29 Backstitch	½

Color numbers given are for Uniek Needloft plastic canvas yarn.

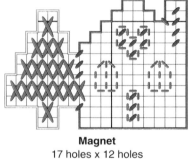

Napkin Ring House
10 holes x 12 holes
Cut 1

COLOR KEY
MAGNET

Plastic Canvas Yarn	Yards
■ Burgundy #03	1
■ Forest #29	2
Uncoded area is eggshell #39 Continental Stitches	2
⁄ Eggshell #39 Overcasting	
⁄ Forest #29 Backstitch	

Color numbers given are for Uniek Needloft plastic canvas yarn.

Magnet
17 holes x 12 holes
Cut 1

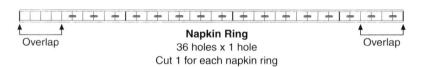

Napkin Ring
36 holes x 1 hole
Cut 1 for each napkin ring

Overlap   Overlap

COLOR KEY
TREE NAPKIN RING

Plastic Canvas Yarn	Yards
■ Forest #29	1
⁄ Eggshell #30 Overcasting	2
⁄ Burgundy #03 Running Stitch	½
○ Attach heart-shaped bead	

Color numbers given are for Uniek Needloft plastic canvas yarn.

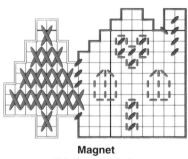

Napkin Ring Tree
8 holes x 11 holes
Cut 1

75 Merry Christmas Projects in Plastic Canvas

Country Rag Basket

Design by Nancy Marshall

A charming decoration for the holidays

Project Notes

Choose fabric with simple, shaded patterns, with a solid color or with an off-white pattern. Avoid multi-colored prints except for fabric with an off-white background.

Prepare strips by marking and clipping selvage edge every ¾". Hold fabric firmly at each cut and pull to tear into strips. Discard first and last strips if they are not ¾"-wide.

Tumble strips in clothes dryer for a few minutes to remove excess lint. Clip extra-long threads from fabric strips.

Fold fabric or use a cut end to thread needle.

Keep fabric strips flat and untwisted while stitching.

Instructions

1 Cut plastic canvas according to graphs (pages 98 and 99). For lining, using plastic canvas pieces as templates, cut poster board slightly smaller than front, back, sides and bottom.

2 Using fabric strips as you would yarn, stitch pieces following graphs.

3 Using sage, Whipstitch basket front and back to sides, then Whipstitch front, back and sides to bottom.

4 Using berry, Whipstitch short edges of handle to top edges of front and back. Overcast all remaining edges with sage.

5 Following manufacturer's directions, fuse webbing to wrong side of lining fabric. Cut fabric ½" larger all around than each poster board piece. Fuse fabric to poster board, folding excess to backside and fusing in place.

6 Glue lined pieces inside basket. ●

Filled with your favorite scented potpourri, this charming basket makes a lovely decoration for any room in your home!

Materials

- ☐ 1 artist-size sheet 5-count plastic canvas
- ☐ ¼ yard berry fabric
- ☐ ½ yard sage fabric
- ☐ Berry/sage print fabric with off-white background: ⅜ yard (for stitching) ½ yard (for lining)
- ☐ #16 tapestry needle
- ☐ Poster board
- ☐ ¼ yard fusible webbing
- ☐ Tacky craft glue

COLOR KEY
Fabric Strips
▨ Berry
▨ Sage
☐ Print on off-white background

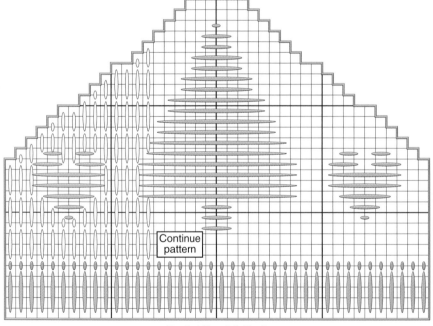

Continue pattern

Basket Front & Back
40 holes x 30 holes
Cut 2

Basket Handle
6 holes x 49 holes
Cut 1

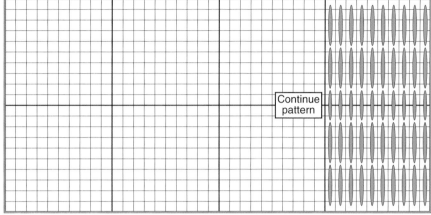

Basket Bottom
40 holes x 20 holes
Cut 1

COLOR KEY
Fabric Strips
▨ Berry
▨ Sage
☐ Print on off-white background

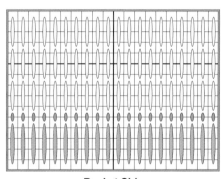

Basket Side
20 holes x 15 holes
Cut 2

Sleepy Mouse Door Hanger

Design by Michele Wilcox

Shhhh! Enjoy the peace of Christmas Eve!

Christmas in the Country

Beginner
Skill Level

You'll enjoy stitching this sweet Christmas door hanger after a peaceful hush has descended upon your house!

Materials

- ☐ ½ sheet 7-count plastic canvas
- ☐ Uniek Needloft plastic canvas yarn as listed in color key
- ☐ #3 pearl cotton as listed in color key
- ☐ #16 tapestry needle

Instructions

1 Cut plastic canvas according to graph.

2 Stitch piece following graph, working uncoded area with beige Continental Stitches.

3 When background stitching is completed, work embroidery with black pearl cotton. Overcast with beige. ●

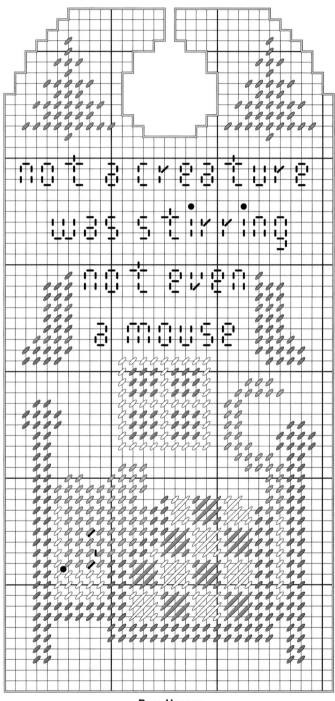

Door Hanger
31 holes x 64 holes
Cut 1

COLOR KEY	
Plastic Canvas Yarn	**Yards**
■ Red #01	5
■ Cinnamon #14	4
■ Holly #27	6
■ Denim #33	1
▨ Gray #38	3
☐ White #41	4
▨ Flesh tone #56	1
Uncoded area is beige #40 Continental Stitches	27
╱ Beige #40 Overcasting	
#3 Pearl Cotton	
╱ Black Backstitch and Straight Stitch	5
● Black French Knot	
Color numbers given are for Uniek Needloft plastic canvas yarn.	

Bear in Heart Basket

Designs by Angie Arickx

Hang up a sweet country bear

Size

2½" W x 3¾" H

Instructions

1 Cut plastic canvas according to graphs; stitch as shown.

2 Using crimson throughout, Whipstitch ends of handle panel together. Whipstitch basket front and back to handle panel; Overcast remaining edges.

3 Glue teddy bear inside basket. ●

Intermediate
Skill Level

Add an enchanting touch to your Christmas trimmings this year with this adorable flocked bear ornament.

Materials

☐ ½ sheet 7-count plastic canvas

☐ Plastic canvas yarn as listed in color key

☐ #16 tapestry needle

☐ 1" flocked brown teddy bear

☐ Hot-glue gun

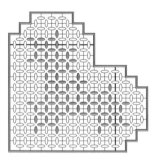

Heart Basket Front & Back
13 holes x 13 holes
Cut 2

COLOR KEY	
Plastic Canvas Yarn	**Yards**
■ Forest #29	3
☐ Eggshell #39	7
■ Crimson #42	5
Color numbers given are for Uniek Needloft plastic canvas yarn.	

Heart Basket Panel
64 holes x 5 holes
Cut 1

A White Christmas

Make your dreams of a white Christmas come true with this collection of snow-loving projects.

BATH 5¢

"Peace" Santa Wreath

Design by Joan Green

This Santa brings peace and beauty

Instructions

1 Cut Santa and star from plastic canvas according to graphs (pages 104 and 106).

2 Stitch star following graph, working uncoded area with deep sea green Continental Stitches. Backstitch letters and work French Knots when background stitching is completed. Overcast with winter white.

3 Stitch Santa following graph, working garland with 2 plies each of deep sea green and dark lagoon. For fur trim on cloak and hood, work winter white stitches first, then stitch over winter white with a double strand of white wispy thread.

COLOR KEY

Worsted Weight Yarn	Yards
■ Medium taupe #8766	1
■ Wood brown #8767	1
■ Deep sea green #8876 and dark lagoon #8822	5
■ Rose #8921	½
□ Winter white #8941	34
□ Light peach #8977	2
Uncoded area on star is deep sea green #8876 Continental Stitches	8
✏ Wood brown #8767 Backstitch	
⅛" Metallic Needlepoint Yarn	
□ White #PC25	9
¹⁄₁₆" Metallic Needlepoint Yarn	
✏ Gold #PM51 Backstitch	10
○ Gold #PM51 French Knot	
Wispy Thread	
■ White #AR2 over winter white #8941	17

Color numbers given are for Spinrite Bernat Berella "4" worsted weight yarn and Rainbow Gallery Plastic Canvas 7 Metallic Needlepoint Yarn, Plastic Canvas 10 Metallic Needlepoint Yarn and Arctic Rays wispy thread.

Beginner
Skill Level

Decorate your Christmas home with this elegant white Santa and coordinating star of peace.

Materials

- □ 1 sheet 7-count plastic canvas
- □ Spinrite Bernat Berella "4" worsted weight yarn as listed in color key
- □ ⅛"-wide Plastic Canvas 7 Metallic Needlepoint Yarn by Rainbow Gallery as listed in color key
- □ ¹⁄₁₆"-wide Plastic Canvas 10 Metallic Needlepoint Yarn by Rainbow Gallery as listed in color key
- □ Arctic Rays wispy thread by Rainbow Gallery as listed in color key
- □ #16 tapestry needle
- □ 5 white roses from Open Rose Garland #222-011-030 by Wrights
- □ White mini-curl doll hair from One & Only Creations
- □ 48" 2½"-wide ivory ribbon with gold wire edge

Continued on page 106

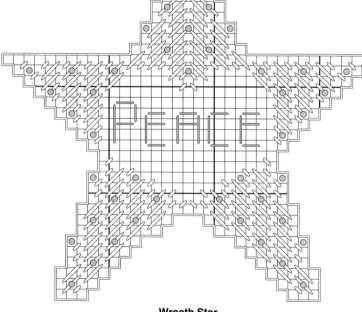

Wreath Star
35 holes x 34 holes
Cut 1

4 When background stitching is completed, work gold French Knots on gown. Backstitch pinecones on garland with 2 plies wood brown. Overcast edges following graph.

5 For gold belt, cut two 9½" lengths of ¹⁄₁₆"-wide gold metallic needlepoint yarn. Place lengths together and thread ends from back to front through holes indicated with blue dots above garland. Make lengths even on front and tie in a knot at waist.

6 Thread ends of double strands from front to back through holes indicated with red dots just above garland, then again from back to front through holes indicated with blue dots just below garland. Tie a knot near end of each double strand; trim ends to resemble tassels. Glue knots to gown.

7 Using photo as a guide throughout, cut bunches of curls from white doll hair and glue on top of beard area. Cut roses from ribbon garland and glue to garland on Santa.

Materials

Continued from page 104

- ☐ 6" floral wire or gold glitter stem
- ☐ 15½" x 17" heart-shaped artificial evergreen wreath
- ☐ Lightweight white poster board
- ☐ Hot-glue gun

8 Using Santa as a template, cut white poster board slightly smaller than Santa, then glue to backside of Santa. Center Santa on wreath and glue to evergreen at top and bottom. Glue star to upper left side of wreath.

9 Make a five-loop bow from wire-edged ribbon; tie floral wire or glitter stem around center of bow. Attach to upper right side of wreath with floral wire or glitter stem. ●

Wreath Santa
49 holes x 85 holes
Cut 1

Mr. Snowman's Bath

Design by Celia Lange Designs

Stitch this whimsical bathroom accent

Cutting & Stitching

1 Cut plastic canvas according to graphs (pages 108 and 109). Cut snowman nose from orange craft foam following pattern given.

2 Stitch pieces following graphs, working uncoded areas on rug with buff Continental Stitches and uncoded background on sign front and back with white Continental Stitches.

3 Work buff French Knots on bath brush front. Work pearl cotton Backstitches on sign front and on head when background stitching is completed.

4 Overcast head, body and arms with adjacent colors. Overcast rug with Windsor blue. Overcast beak area on rubber duck with vibrant orange and remaining edges with bright yellow.

Assembly

1 Use photo as a guide through out assembly. Using dark spruce throughout, Whipstitch wrong sides of sign front and back together along top edges; Overcast remaining edges. Whipstitch wrong sides of bath brush front and back together.

2 Glue a layer of packing peanuts in bottom of tub. Glue snowman body between peanuts, then add and glue another layer of packing peanuts. Glue marbles over packing peanuts.

3 Glue nose to head, then glue head and arms to body. Glue bath brush to hand on raised arm. Glue rubber duck to marbles.

4 Glue washtub and sign to rug. Put broom handle through tub handle and glue in place.

5 Wrap and glue ribbon around top hat, then glue two pinecones with berries to hat over ribbon. Glue hat to rug in front of tub. Glue remaining two pinecones with berries to top of sign.

6 Cut white terry cloth to form towel and washcloth. Fringe towel and hang over remaining tub handle; glue in place. Crumple washcloth and glue to lower hand. ●

Mr. Snowman's Bath

Beginner
Skill Level

Your holiday guests will chuckle when they see this delightful project on a shelf in your bathroom!

Materials

- ☐ 1 sheet Darice Ultra Stiff 7-count plastic canvas
- ☐ Coats & Clark Red Heart Super Saver worsted weight yarn Art. E301 as listed in color key
- ☐ Darice Bright Pearls pearlized metallic cord as listed in color key
- ☐ DMC #3 pearl cotton as listed in color key
- ☐ #16 tapestry needle
- ☐ Small amount orange Fun Foam craft foam by Westrim Crafts
- ☐ 5½" x 2" oval galvanized metal washtub with handles
- ☐ White plastic foam packing peanuts
- ☐ 45–50 (14mm) clear luster marbles
- ☐ 2" x 1¼" black plastic top hat
- ☐ 4½" of ¼"-wide red satin ribbon
- ☐ 4" miniature broom
- ☐ 4 miniature frosted pinecones with berries

Continued on page 109

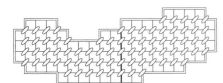

Snowman Arm
19 holes x 7 holes
Cut 2

Snowman Nose

COLOR KEY	
Worsted Weight Yarn	**Yards**
■ Dark spruce #361	14
■ Windsor blue #380	13
☐ Bright yellow #324	1
Uncoded area on sign is white #311 Continental Stitches	5
Uncoded areas on rug are buff #334 Continental Stitches	14
✏ Vibrant orange #354 Ocercasting	¼
● Buff #334 French Knot	
Pearlized Metallic Cord	
☐ White #3410-01	19
#3 Pearl Cotton	
✏ Black #310 Backstitch	1
✏ Dark antique blue #930 Backstitch	1
Color numbers given are for Red Heart Super Saver worsted weight yarn Art. E301 and DMC #3 pearl cotton.	

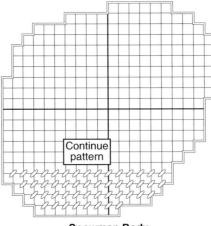

Continue pattern

Snowman Body
20 holes x 20 holes
Cut 1

75 Merry Christmas Projects in Plastic Canvas

COLOR KEY

Worsted Weight Yarn	Yards
▨ Dark spruce #361	14
▨ Windsor blue #380	13
☐ Bright yellow #324	1
Uncoded area on sign is white #311 Continental Stitches	5
Uncoded areas on rug are buff #334 Continental Stitches	14
⁄ Vibrant orange #354 Ocercasting	¼
● Buff #334 French Knot	

Pearlized Metallic Cord

☐ White #3410-01	19

#3 Pearl Cotton

⁄ Black #310 Backstitch	1
⁄ Dark antique blue #930 Backstitch	1

Color numbers given are for Red Heart Super Saver worsted weight yarn Art. E301 and DMC #3 pearl cotton.

Materials

Continued from page 108

- ☐ Scrap white terry cloth
- ☐ Hot-glue gun and Crafty Super Strength glue sticks from Adhesive Technologies Inc.

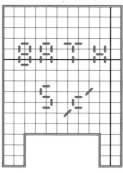

Sign Front & Back
11 holes x 15 holes
Cut 2
Stitch embroidery on front only

Rubber Duck
7 holes x 6 holes
Cut 1

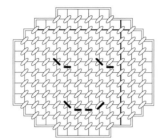

Snowman Head
13 holes x 12 holes
Cut 1

Bath Brush Front
3 holes x 11 holes
Cut 1

Bath Brush Back
3 holes x 11 holes
Cut 1

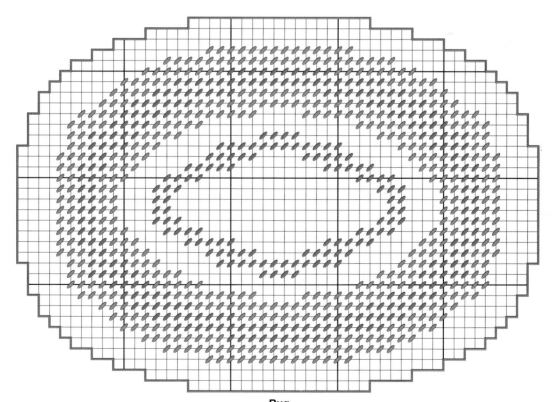

Rug
49 holes x 35 holes
Cut 1

Sparkling Snowflakes

Design by Angie Arickx

Perfect snowflakes with sparkle and shine

Intermediate
Skill Level

Hung from a doorway and in a window, this three-dimensional snowflake ornament and suncatcher pair brings the beauty of a fresh snowfall indoors!

Materials

- ☐ 4 (5") plastic canvas hexagon shapes by Uniek
- ☐ ⅛"-wide Plastic Canvas 7 Metallic Needlepoint Yarn by Rainbow Gallery as listed in color key
- ☐ #16 tapestry needle
- ☐ Suction cup with hook

Instructions

1 Cut hanging loops from two hexagons, leaving hanging loops on remaining two hexagons intact. Cut snowflake shapes from all four hexagons according to graph (page 120), cutting away gray areas. Cut the two snowflakes without hanging loops in half where indicated on graph.

2 Stitch and Overcast pieces following graphs, leaving long straight edges of each half unstitched. For suncatcher, work white pearl stitches over center bar indicated with yellow. Do not work stitches over center bar on remaining whole snowflake, which will be used for doorway ornament.

3 Hang suncatcher in window with suction cup as desired.

4 For doorway ornament, Whipstitch straight edges of two snowflake halves to each side of remaining whole snowflake along its unstitched center seam.

5 Evenly spread out edges of ornament and hang as desired. ●

Graph on page 120

Snow Globe Coasters

Design by Celia Lange Designs

Stitch the beauty of winter's first snow

Instructions

1 Cut plastic canvas according to graphs. Cut one 21-hole x 9-hole piece for holder bottom.

2 Stitch pieces following graphs, working uncoded areas on coasters with blue jewel Continental Stitches. Work holder bottom with brown Continental Stitches.

3 When background stitching is completed, work pearl ribbon embroidery on globes.

4 For coasters, Overcast stands with brown and globes with blue jewel. For holder, using mid brown, Whipstitch front and back to sides. With brown, Whipstitch front, back and sides to bottom; Overcast top edges.

5 Cut white craft foam slightly smaller than coasters, then glue to backsides. ●

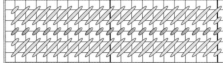

Holder Side
9 holes x 6 holes
Cut 2

Holder Front & Back
21 holes x 6 holes
Cut 2

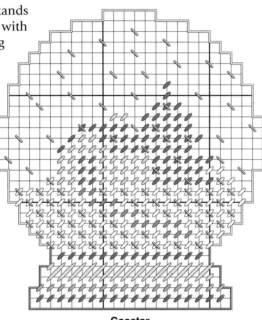

Coaster
25 holes x 28 holes
Cut 4

COLOR KEY

Worsted Weight Yarn	Yards
☐ White #1	13
☐ Yellow #230	1
◼ Brown #328	14
☐ Warm brown #336	3
☐ Mid brown #339	12
◼ Nickel #401	2
◼ Dark sage #633	4
◼ Skipper blue #848	2
◼ Cherry red #912	1
Uncoded areas are blue jewel #818 Continental Sitches	27
✎ Blue jewel #818 Overcasting	
Heavy (#32) Braid	
☐ Gold #002	7
⅛" Ribbon	
✎ Pearl #032 Backstitch and Straight Stitch	12

Color numbers given are for Red Heart Classic worsted weight yarn Art. E267 and Super Saver worsted weight yarn Art. E301, and Kreinik Heavy (#32) Braid and ⅛" Ribbon.

Snow Globe Coasters

Beginner
Skill Level

Stitch this set of scenic coasters for your holiday entertaining

Materials

- ☐ 1 sheet Darice Ultra Stiff 7-count plastic canvas
- ☐ Coats & Clark Red Heart Classic worsted weight yarn Art. E267 as listed in color key
- ☐ Coats & Clark Red Heart Super Saver worsted weight yarn Art. E301 as listed in color key
- ☐ Kreinik Heavy (#32) Braid as listed in color key
- ☐ Kreinik ⅛" Ribbon as listed in color key
- ☐ #16 tapestry needle
- ☐ Sheet white Fun Foam craft foam by Westrim Crafts
- ☐ Hot-glue gun

75 Merry Christmas Projects in Plastic Canvas

Snowman Place Cards

Design by Alida Macor

Beginner
Skill Level

Seat your Christmas dinner guests with these darling Mr. and Mrs. Snowman place cards.

Materials

- ☐ ½ sheet white 7-count plastic canvas
- ☐ Small amount red 7-count plastic canvas
- ☐ Small amount green 7-count plastic canvas
- ☐ Uniek Needloft plastic canvas yarn as listed in color key
- ☐ #16 tapestry needle
- ☐ 4 (6mm) black beads
- ☐ ½" white pompom
- ☐ 9" of ⅛"-wide red satin ribbon
- ☐ 9" of ⅛"-wide green satin ribbon
- ☐ Sewing needle and white sewing thread
- ☐ White unruled index card
- ☐ Craft glue (optional)

Easy-to-stitch place cards

Instructions

1 Cut two snowmen and two stands from white plastic canvas; cut two red hat pieces and two red mittens from red plastic canvas; cut two green hat pieces and two green mittens from green plastic canvas according to graphs (page 114). Stands will remain unstitched.

2 Stitch snowmen following graph, leaving neck areas unstitched at this time.

3 Using Half Cross Stitches and following graphs, stitch two mittens with Christmas green and two mittens with Christmas red, reversing one mitten of each color before stitching.

4 Using mitten color, Whipstitch one pair of mittens to sides of each snowman from blue dot to blue dot.

5 For each snowman, center one unstitched stand on wrong side of snowman body. Using

Snowman Place Cards

white throughout, Whipstitch top edge of stand to unstitched neck of snowman with a Continental Stitch. Whipstitch shoulder areas of stand and snowman together; Overcast all remaining edges.

6 Stitch hats following graphs. Using adjacent colors, Whipstitch wrong sides of corresponding hat pieces together around sides and top. Overcast bottom edges. Sew or glue white pompom to center top of red hat.

7 Using sewing needle and white thread, sew beads for eyes to snowmen heads where indicated on graph. Using photo as a guide, glue green hat to snowman with

green mittens and red hat to snowman with red mittens.

8 Tie red ribbon in a bow around neck of snowman with green hat and mittens. Tie green ribbon in a bow around neck of snowman with red hat and mittens.

9 Cut one 2½" x ½" strip from index card for each snowman. Print desired name on strips and place behind tops of mittens as in photo. ●

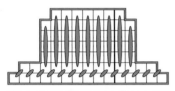

Place Card Snowman Green Hat
15 holes x 7 holes
Cut 2 from green

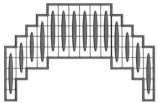

Place Card Snowman Red Hat
14 holes x 9 holes
Cut 2 from red

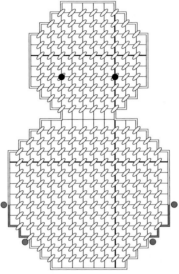

Place Card Snowman
15 holes x 25 holes
Cut 2 from white

Place Card Snowman Mitten
3 holes x 4 holes
Cut 2, reverse 1, from green
Stitch as graphed
Cut 2, reverse 1, from red
Stitch with Christmas red

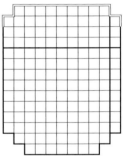

Place Card Snowman Stand
11 holes x 14 holes
Cut 2 from white
Do not stitch

COLOR KEY

Plastic Canvas Yarn	Yards
■ Christmas red #02	4
■ Christmas green #28	4
□ White #41	16
● Attach bead	

Color numbers given are for Uniek Needloft plastic canvas yarn.

Snowball Stand
Tissue Topper

Design by Celia Lange Designs

Don't miss out on this holiday special!

This colorful tissue-box cover will add cheer and whimsy to the season!

Cutting & Stitching

1 Cut plastic canvas according to graphs (pages 116 and 117).

2 Stitch pieces following graphs, working uncoded areas on snowman head, signs and awnings with white Continental Stitches. Work only two topper sides with snowmen. Stitch remaining two sides without snowmen, working top portions entirely with the blue jewel pattern.

3 Following graphs, Overcast "Holiday Special" signs with cherry red and emerald green candy-cane stripes. Overcast snowman heads, snowball signs and "5¢" signs with white. Work black pearl cotton embroidery on snowman heads and bodies and on signs.

4 Overcast hats with black. Work a cherry red Straight Stitch on each hat, securing ends on backside.

Assembly

1 Use photo as a guide through out assembly. With cherry red, Whipstitch side edges of corresponding awning pieces together, then Overcast top edges. Overcast bottom edges with emerald green.

2 Using cherry red throughout, Overcast inside edges of top, then work a Straight Stitch in each corner. Whipstitch topper sides together with Cross Stitches, alternating snowman sides with blue jewel sides; Whipstitch top to sides. Overcast bottom edges with paddy green.

3 Cut four 6" lengths cherry red yarn. Secure two lengths under stitching on backside of each "Holiday Special" sign.

4 Center yarn on opposite sides of top awning; thread through stitching on backside, allowing about ½" between signs and bottom edges of awning. Trim excess yarn.

5 Slip awning over tissue topper, making sure top edges are even and placing signs over blue jewel sides. Glue awning to topper. Glue signs to sides.

6 Glue table awning to tissue topper, placing top edge along cherry red line on sides.

7 Glue snowman heads to snowman bodies, then glue hats to heads and sides. Glue "5¢" signs to toothpicks; then glue signs and toothpicks to the left of snowmen.

8 Center and glue snowball signs under table awning on snowman sides. Glue pompoms in stacks of snowballs to each side. ●

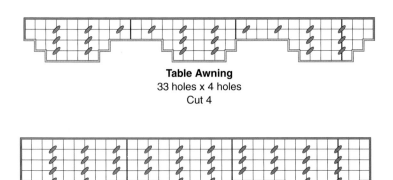

Table Awning
33 holes x 4 holes
Cut 4

Top Awning
33 holes x 6 holes
Cut 4

Snowball Stand Tissue Topper

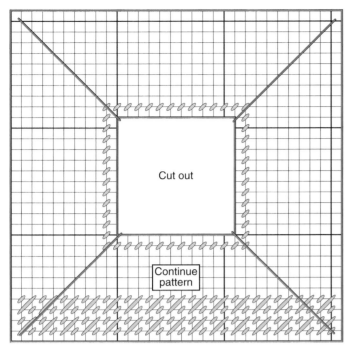

Tissue Topper Top
31 holes x 31 holes
Cut 1

Cut out

Continue pattern

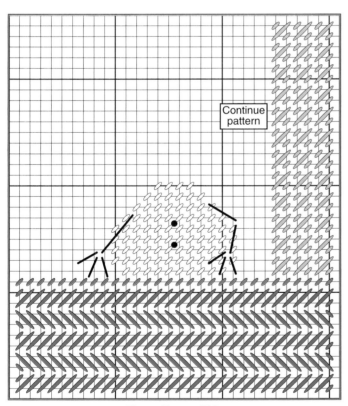

Tissue Topper Side
31 holes x 36 holes
Cut 4
Stitch 2 with snowman
Stitch 2 without snowman

Continue pattern

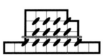

Snowman Hat
9 holes x 4 holes
Cut 2

Snowman Head
7 holes x 7 holes
Cut 2

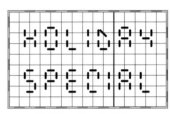

Holiday Special Sign
15 holes x 9 holes
Cut 2

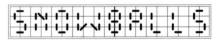

Snowball Sign
19 holes x 3 holes
Cut 2

5¢ Sign
5 holes x 4 holes
Cut 2

COLOR KEY

Worsted Weight Yarn	Yards
☐ White #1	27
■ Black #12	2
▨ Paddy green #686	8
☐ Blue jewel #818	26
▨ Cherry red #912	64
Uncoded areas are white	23
#1 Continental Stitches	

⟋ Emerald green #676 Overcasting
⟋ Cherry red #912 Straight Stitch

#3 Pearl Cotton

⟋ Black #310 Backstitch and Straight Stitch	12
● Black #310 French Knot	

Color numbers given are for Red Heart Classic worsted weight yarn Art. E267 and DMC #3 pearl cotton.

Cheery Snowman Picture

Design by Kimberly A. Suber

Brighten a corner of your home

Beginner
Skill Level

Dress up a door or wall in your home with this bright and cheery snowman picture!

Materials

- ☐ 1 sheet 7-count plastic canvas
- ☐ Worsted weight yarn as listed in color key
- ☐ Metallic cord as listed in color key
- ☐ 6-strand embroidery floss as listed in color key
- ☐ #16 tapestry needle
- ☐ 5 (⅜") black 4-hole buttons
- ☐ 7" x 8½" piece felt in coordinating color
- ☐ Hot-glue gun

COLOR KEY

Worsted Weight Yarn	Yards
☐ White	10
☐ Green	3
☐ Red	3
■ Black	2
☐ Brown	1
Uncoded area is royal blue Continental Stitches	20
✏ Black Backstitch and Straight Stitch	
✏ Orange Backstitch	1
✏ Pink Straight Stitch	1
● Black French Knot	
Metallic Cord	
☐ Silver	1
6-Strand Embroidery Floss	
✏ White Straight Stitch	6
○ White French Knot	
● Attach button	

Instructions

1 Cut plastic canvas according to graph.

2 Stitch piece following graph, working uncoded area with royal blue Continental Stitches. Work embroidery when background stitching is completed. Overcast with red.

3 Using 2 plies white yarn, Cross-Stitch buttons to snow-man where indicated on graph.

4 For hanger, cut desired lengths of red and green yarn. Twist lengths together and glue ends to top corners on backside of picture. Glue felt to backside of piece over hanger ends. ●

A White Christmas

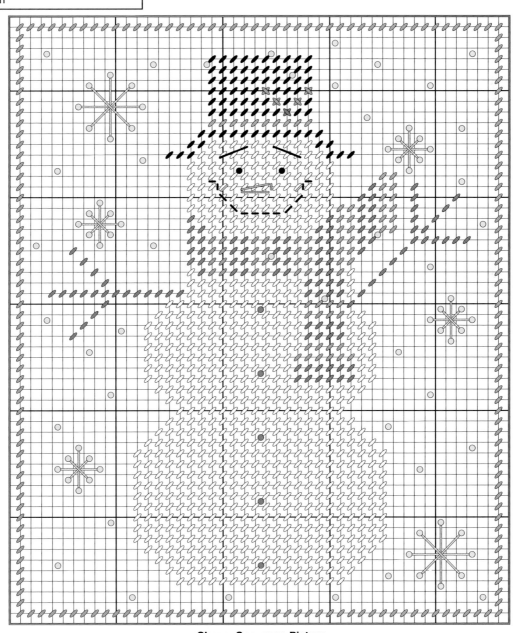

Cheery Snowman Picture
47 holes x 57 holes
Cut 1

Sparkling Snowflakes

Continued from page 110

COLOR KEY	
⅛" Metallic Needlepoint Yarn	Yards
☐ White pearl #PC10	38
✐ White pearl #PC10 Backstitch	
Color number given is for Rainbow Gallery Plastic Canvas 7 Metallic Needlepoint Yarn.	

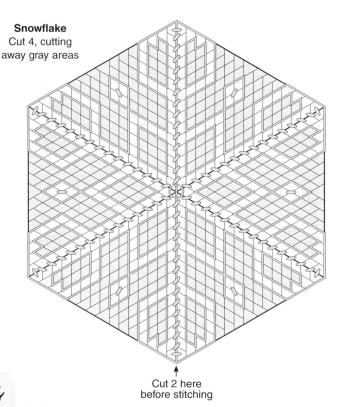

Snowflake
Cut 4, cutting
away gray areas

↑
Cut 2 here
before stitching

Gingerbread Cutout Cookies

By Shelly Vaughan

Touch of Pineapple Gingerbread People

Cookies
½ cup butter-flavored shortening
1 cup sugar
1 cup dark molasses
1 cup pineapple juice or more as needed
5 cups flour
2 teaspoons baking soda
1 teaspoon salt
1½ teaspoons ground ginger
1 teaspoon cinnamon
1 teaspoon ground cloves
1 teaspoon ground nutmeg
Miniature candy-coated chocolate candies and/or raisins

Icing
1½ cups confectioners' sugar
2 tablespoons pineapple juice

1 For cookies, combine shortening, sugar and molasses in large bowl. Stir in pineapple juice. In another bowl, stir together flour, baking soda, salt, ginger, cinnamon, cloves and nutmeg. Gradually stir into molasses mixture until thoroughly incorporated. (Dough will be stiff.) Cover and chill for 2 hours.

2 Preheat oven to 350 degrees. Spray cookie sheet with non-stick cooking spray once.

3 On floured surface, roll dough out ¼ inch thick. Cut into desired shapes with floured cookie cutter, using gingerbread people cutter or other cutter. Place cookies 1"–2" apart on prepared cookie sheet. Decorate with candies and/or raisins as desired. Bake for 10 minutes, or until light finger indentation springs back. Cool slightly.

4 For icing, combine confectioners' sugar and pineapple juice in small bowl. Pipe onto cookies as desired. Cool completely.

5 Store cookies in single layer in airtight container, or layer cookies with waxed paper separating layers. Makes 3 dozen. ❤

Decorating Gingerbread Cookie Tips

❤ Gently press decorating candies or other items into cookies before baking.

❤ Pipe icing onto warm cookies with a small decorating tip.

❤ If you do not have a pastry bag and decorating tips, spoon icing into a small plastic bag. Cut a very small tip off one corner.

❤ Icing is quick and easy to make. If you prefer convenience items, however, you may use tubes of decorating icing with decorating tips.

❤ Roll pastry bag or plastic bag down from top as you pipe.

❤ If you would like to add some color to your cookies, lightly sprinkle colored sugars, sprinkles, nonpareils or flaked coconut over wet icing. Gently shake off any excess, if necessary.

Christmas Wrappings

This holiday season, give two gifts in one by stitching a festive gift bag or basket in which to tuck your most special holiday surprises!

A bright and colorful bag for gift-giving

Instructions

1 Cut tree and gift packages from regular plastic canvas; cut latch pieces and bag pieces from stiff plastic canvas according to graphs (pages 123 and 124).

2 Stitch pieces following graphs. For bag back, do not stitch tree trunk and tree skirt; stitch mid brown and cornmeal patterns only. Do not stitch darts closed on bag sides at this time.

3 Overcast tree with dark sage. Work Backstitches on tree with dark sage, then work French Knots in colors indicated.

4 Overcast gift packages with adjacent colors. Using photo as a guide, wrap desired color of yarn around each package, tying a small bow along top edge.

Assembly

1 Using cornmeal, Cross-Stitch darts closed on bag sides, following graphs. Using adjacent colors, Whipstitch bag front and back to bag sides. Whipstitch front, back and sides to bottom with mid brown.

2 Using cornmeal throughout, Whipstitch top edge of lower latch to bottom edge of upper latch, then Overcast around sides and bottom of assembled latch. With wrong sides facing, Whipstitch top edge of latch to center top edge of bag back, Overcast remaining top edges while Whipstitching.

3 Using photo as a guide, glue tree and gift packages to bag front. Sew star to bag just above treetop with cornmeal. Tie elastic cord in a loop, making sure loop is large enough to fit over button.

4 Thread ends of elastic cord from front to back where indicated on lower latch, pulling cord so loop knot is next to stitching. Tie in a knot on backside; thread ends under stitching. Glue to secure.

5 For handle, thread ends of 1-yard length of gold metallic cord from front to back where indicated on one side. Pull one end across inside front of bag to other side of bag.

6 Thread end through hole to outside of bag, then thread end through remaining hole to inside of bag. Pull cord across inside back of bag. Tie ends in a knot and glue to inside of bag side. ●

Beginner
Skill Level

Any recipient is sure to love this fun and festive Christmas tree bag!

Materials

- ☐ 2 sheets Darice Ultra Stiff 7-count plastic canvas
- ☐ 1 sheet regular 7-count plastic canvas
- ☐ Coats & Clark Red Heart Classic worsted weight yarn Art. E267 as listed in color key
- ☐ #16 tapestry needle
- ☐ 1 yard Darice Bright Jewels gold #3411-01 metallic cord
- ☐ ¾" (19mm) gold metallic shank star button
- ☐ Small amount gold elastic cording
- ☐ Hot-glue gun

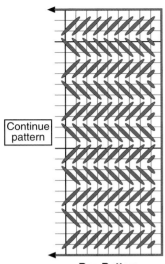

Bag Bottom
39 holes x 23 holes
Cut 1 from stiff

Continue pattern

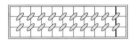

Upper Latch
11 holes x 3 holes
Cut 1 from stiff

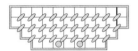

Lower Latch
11 holes x 4 holes
Cut 1 from stiff

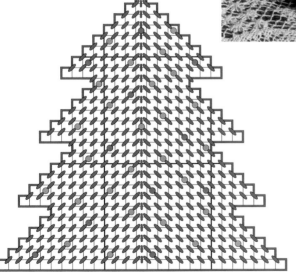

Christmas Tree
27 holes x 26 holes
Cut 1 from regular

COLOR KEY	
Plastic Canvas Yarn	**Yards**
▢ Cornmeal #220	75
▣ Mid brown #339	30
▣ Coffee #365	1
▣ Dark sage #633	9
▢ Honey gold #645	1
▣ Emerald green #676	1
▣ True blue #822	1
▢ Cherry red #912	1
▣ Cardinal #917	3
╱ Dark sage #633 Backstitch	
✕ Cornmeal #220 Cross Stitch	
● Honey gold #645 French Knot	
● Emerald green #676 French Knot	
● True blue #822 French Knot	
● Cherry red #912 French Knot	
○ Attach loop	
● Attach handle	

Color numbers given are for Red Heart Classic worsted weight yarn Art. E267.

Christmas Wrappings

Christmas Tree Gift Bag

Gift Packages

5 holes x 4 holes
Cut 1 from regular

4 holes x 5 holes
Cut 1 from regular

5 holes x 7 holes
Cut 2 from regular
Stitch 1 as graphed
Stitch 1 with emerald green

5 holes x 5 holes
Cut 2 from regular
Stitch 1 as graphed
Stitch 1 with honey gold

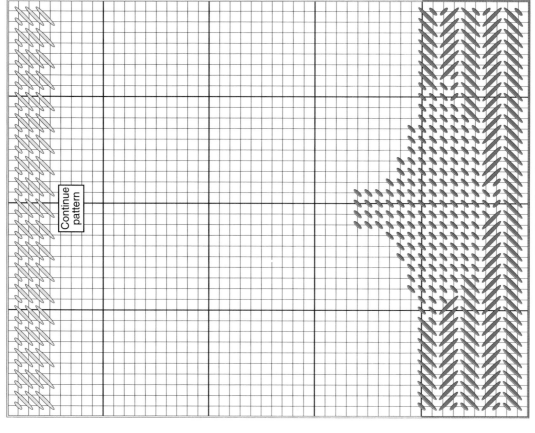

Bag Front & Back
39 holes x 49 holes
Cut 2 from stiff
Stitch front as graphed
Stitch back with mid brown
and cornmeal patterns only

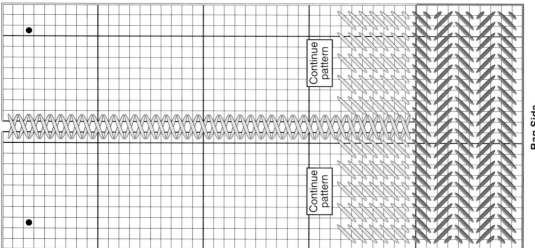

Bag Side
23 holes x 49 holes
Cut 2 from stiff

Poinsettia Gift Bag

By Angie Arickx

Just the right size for a very special gift

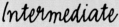

Intermediate
Skill Level

Create this artistic poinsettia gift bag to give to a friend, family member or co-worker.

Materials

- ☐ 4 (5") plastic canvas stars by Uniek
- ☐ ¼ sheet 7-count plastic canvas
- ☐ Uniek Needloft plastic canvas yarn as listed in color key
- ☐ #16 tapestry needle
- ☐ Hot-glue gun

Instructions

1 Following graphs (page 126), cut poinsettias from two plastic canvas stars, cutting away gray areas. Do not cut two remaining stars, which will be used for bag front and back. Cut bag handle, bag sides, bow and bow bands from 7-count plastic canvas according to graphs (page 126).

2 Using yellow throughout, Overcast bow and top and bottom edges of bow band pieces. Whip-handle and poinsettias following graphs. Work yellow French Knots on poinsettias when background stitching is completed.

stitch wrong sides of the two band pieces together along side edges.

3 Stitch bag front and back (page 126), bag sides, bag

4 Using Christmas green throughout, Whipstitch top and bottom edges of side pieces together, forming one long strip. Overcast bag handle.

5 With forest, Whipstitch sides to bag front and back around sides and bottom from blue dot to blue dot; Overcast top edges of bag front and back. Overcast top edges of sides with Christmas green.

6 Using photo as a guide through step 8, glue poinsettias to bag front and back.

7 Glue right side of one handle end to top inside left corner of bag front, then glue right side of remaining handle end to top inside corner on opposite side of bag back.

8 Center and glue bow to band front. Place band over top points of bag, then glue band back to bag back. Top point of bag front can be slipped in and out of band. ●

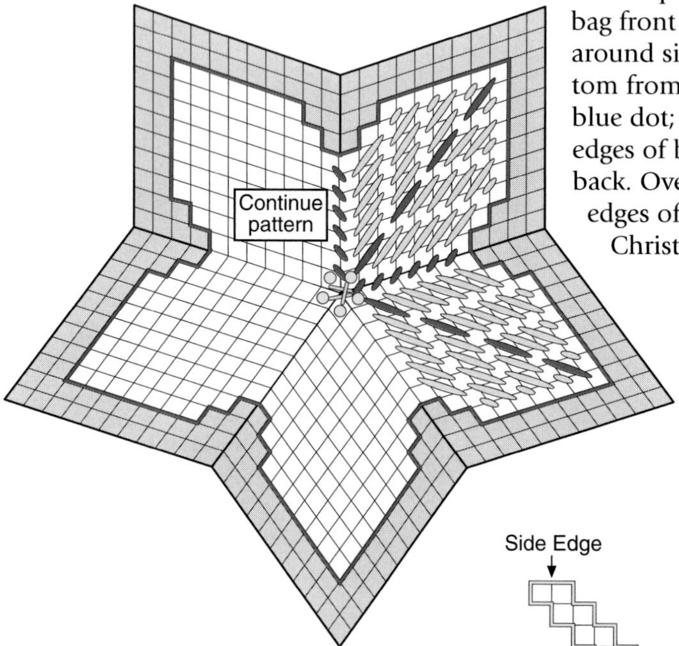

Poinsettia
Cut 2
Cut away shaded gray area

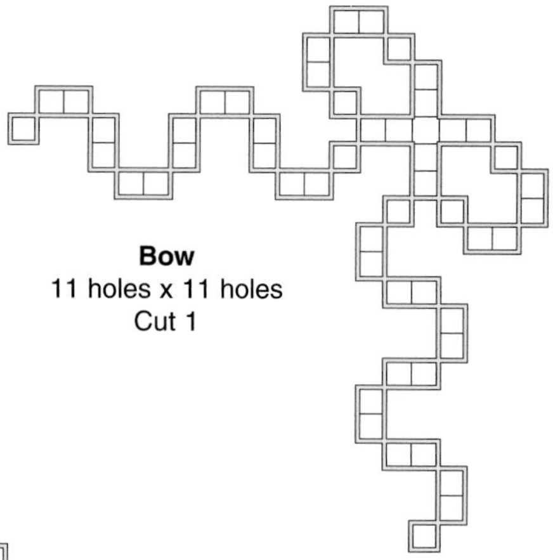

Bow
11 holes x 11 holes
Cut 1

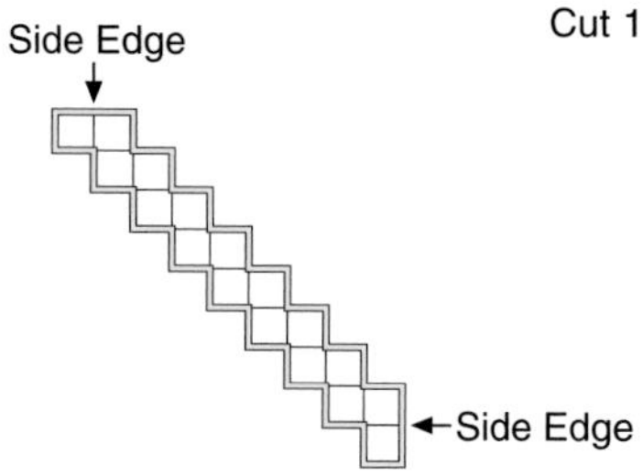

Side Edge

←Side Edge

Bow Band
9 holes x 9 holes
Cut 2

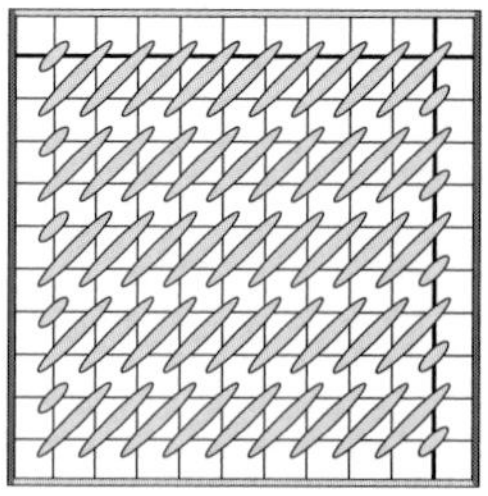

Bag Side
11 holes x 11 holes
Cut 6

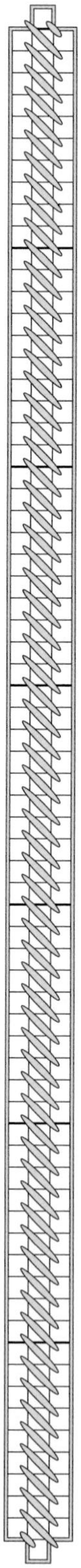

Bag Handle
71 holes x 3 holes
Cut 1

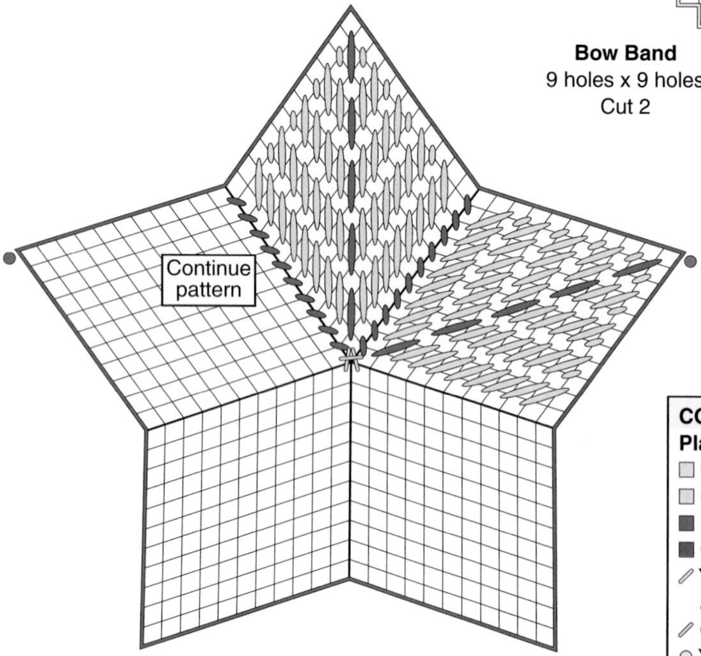

Bag Front & Back
Stitch 2

COLOR KEY	
Plastic Canvas Yarn	**Yards**
☐ Christmas red #02	5
☐ Christmas green #28	33
■ Forest #29	9
■ Crimson #42	4
⁄ Yellow #57 Overcasting and Whipstitching	5
⁄ Christmas green #28 Straight Stitch	
○ Yellow #57 French Knot	
Color numbers given are for Uniek Needloft plastic canvas yarn.	

75 Merry Christmas Projects in Plastic Canvas

Patchwork Tree Basket

Design by Vicki Blizzard

Fill this large basket with a dozen gifts

Cutting & Stitching

1 From clear plastic canvas, cut one basket front, one basket back and one basket handle according to graphs (pages 129–131). Also cut two 59-hole x 34-hole pieces for basket sides.

2 From red plastic canvas, cut one basket front according to graph. Also cut one 59-hole x 59-hole piece for basket bottom and three 59-hole x 34-hole pieces for basket back and sides. All plastic canvas pieces will remain unstitched for lining.

3 For star sections, cut five diamond shapes from plastic canvas star according to graph (page 131).

4 Following graphs (pages 130 and 131), cut hexagons into 18 tree triangles, one large tree trunk and nine small tree trunks, rounding off points.

5 Stitch tree trunks following graphs. Overcast with walnut. Stitch tree triangles as desired using the 10 patterns given. Overcast each with brisk green.

6 Stitch and Overcast star sections following graphs, working gold medium (#16) braid embroidery when background stitching and Overcasting are completed.

7 Stitch clear plastic canvas basket front, back and handle following graphs, overlapping five holes on ends of basket handle with handle strips on basket front and back before stitching handle. Stitch clear plastic canvas sides with almond, following pattern given for basket front and back.

Assembly

1 Place unstitched lining pieces behind corresponding stitched basket pieces. Using almond and two stitches per hole as needed through step 2, Whipstitch sides to front and back through all four thicknesses, then Whipstitch front, back and sides to unstitched bottom.

2 Whipstitch remaining edges of basket and liner pieces together; Overcast handle.

3 Using a small amount of glue, glue edges of white diamond shapes together to form a star (Fig. 1). With gold medium (#16) braid, work two Straight Stitches connecting star sections.

Fig. 1

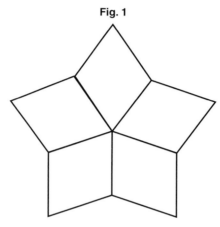

4 Using a small amount of glue, glue edges of nine triangles together to form a large tree, then glue large tree trunk to center bottom triangle (Fig. 2). With gold medium (#16) braid, work four to five Straight Stitches connecting tree sections.

Fig. 2

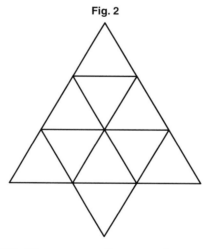

5 Glue one small tree trunk to center bottom of each remaining tree triangle.

Patchwork Tree Basket

Advanced
Skill Level

Turn this festive basket into a decorative gift by filling it with pinecones, pine boughs and holly!

Materials

- ☐ 4 (5") plastic canvas hexagon shapes by Uniek
- ☐ 5" plastic canvas star by Uniek
- ☐ 3 sheets Uniek Quick-Count clear 7-count plastic canvas
- ☐ 3 sheets Uniek Quick-Count red 7-count plastic canvas
- ☐ Spinrite plastic canvas yarn as listed in color key
- ☐ Kreinik Medium (#16) Braid as listed in color key
- ☐ #16 tapestry needle
- ☐ #22 tapestry needle
- ☐ 1½ yards of ⅛"-wide red satin ribbon
- ☐ 18" of 1"-wide red grosgrain ribbon
- ☐ 19 (10.5mm x 10mm) ruby heart-shaped cabochons from The Beadery
- ☐ ½"–1" assorted red buttons
- ☐ Hot-glue gun

Overlap with handle

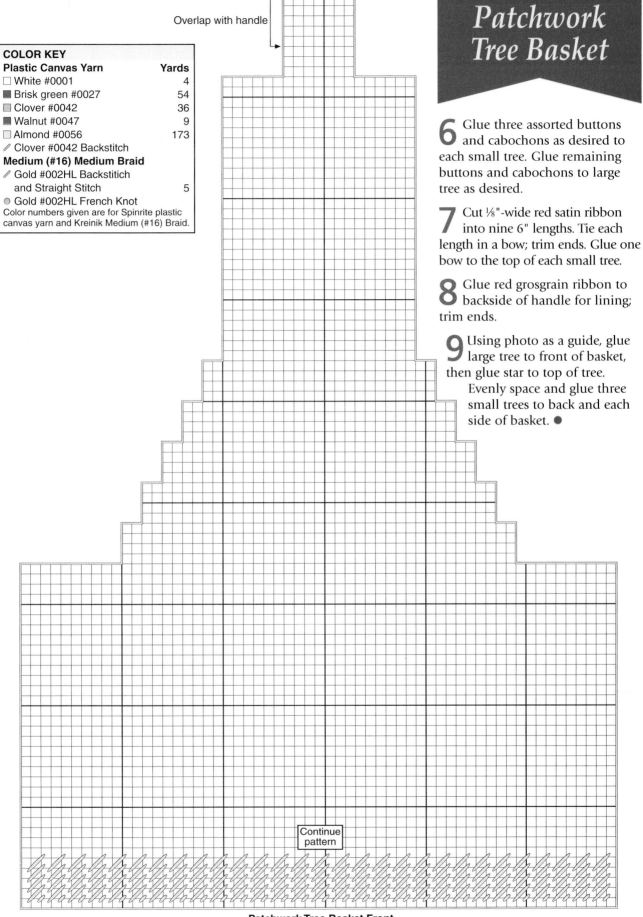

COLOR KEY

Plastic Canvas Yarn	Yards
☐ White #0001	4
■ Brisk green #0027	54
☐ Clover #0042	36
■ Walnut #0047	9
☐ Almond #0056	173
∕ Clover #0042 Backstitch	
Medium (#16) Medium Braid	
∕ Gold #002HL Backstitich and Straight Stitch	5
⊙ Gold #002HL French Knot	

Color numbers given are for Spinrite plastic canvas yarn and Kreinik Medium (#16) Braid.

6 Glue three assorted buttons and cabochons as desired to each small tree. Glue remaining buttons and cabochons to large tree as desired.

7 Cut ⅛"-wide red satin ribbon into nine 6" lengths. Tie each length in a bow; trim ends. Glue one bow to the top of each small tree.

8 Glue red grosgrain ribbon to backside of handle for lining; trim ends.

9 Using photo as a guide, glue large tree to front of basket, then glue star to top of tree. Evenly space and glue three small trees to back and each side of basket. ●

Continue pattern

Patchwork Tree Basket Front
59 holes x 90 holes
Cut 1 from clear
Stitch as graphed
Cut 1 from red
Do not stitch

Christmas Wrappings 129

Patchwork Tree Basket

Overlap with handle

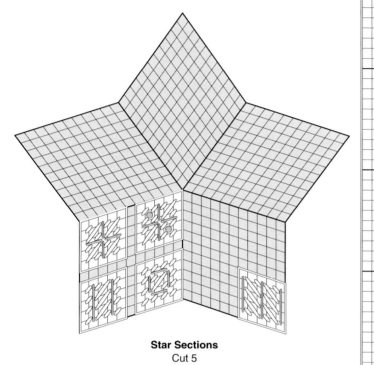

Star Sections
Cut 5

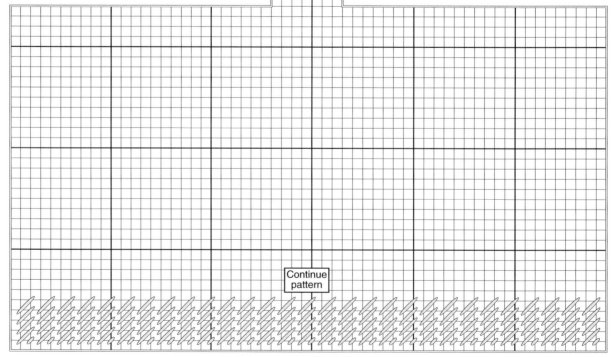

Continue pattern

Patchwork Tree Basket Back
59 holes x 90 holes
Cut 1 from clear

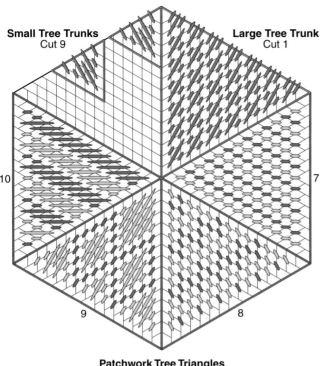

Small Tree Trunks
Cut 9

Large Tree Trunk
Cut 1

10

7

9

8

Patchwork Tree Triangles
Cut apart before stitching

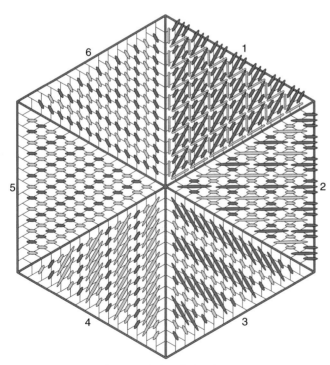

6

1

5

2

4

3

Patchwork Tree Triangles
Cut 18 apart before stitching
Stitch patterns 1-10 as desired

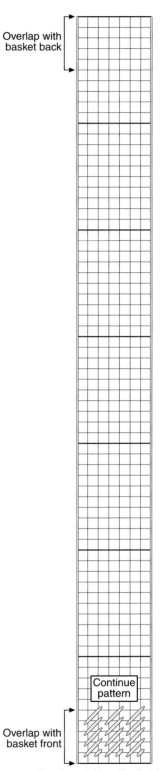

Overlap with
basket back

Continue
pattern

Overlap with
basket front

Patchwork Tree Basket Handle
7 holes x 70 holes
Cut 1 from clear

Snowbirdie Box

Design by Janelle Giese

This box makes a charming decoration

Cutting

1 Cut all bird, hat and scarf pieces from regular plastic canvas; cut all box and post pieces from stiff plastic canvas according to graphs (pages 134 and 135).

2 From regular plastic canvas, cut two 2-hole x 3-hole pieces for leg sides and two 3-hole x 3-hole pieces for legs front and back.

3 From stiff plastic canvas, cut one 11-hole x 11-hole piece for post top, one 21-hole x 21-hole piece for box bottom and four 3-hole x 19-hole pieces for lid lips. Lid lips and box bottom will remain unstitched.

Snowbirdie

Stitching & Assembly

1 With beige, Continental Stitch front, back and sides of legs. Whipstitch front and back to sides, forming a box. Stitch and Overcast feet following graph. Whipstitch legs to feet where indicated on graph.

2 Stitch face, head back, head gusset and beak following graphs. Work three Straight Stitches for each eye with black pearl cotton. Cross Stitch cheeks with 2 strands rose embroidery floss.

3 With beige, Overcast around sides and bottom of beak from beige dot to beige dot, then Whipstitch top edge to face where indicated on graph.

4 Using sail blue throughout, Whipstitch top and bottom

darts on face closed. Matching red triangles, Whipstitch head gusset around sides and top of face. Whipstitch gusset around sides and top of head back.

5 Stitch back, sides and body gusset following graphs, reversing one side before stitching. When background stitching is completed, work black pearl cotton Backstitches on sides.

6 With sail blue, Whipstitch top edge of legs to body gusset where indicated on graph. With wrong sides facing, Whipstitch tail edges of sides together from blue dot to blue dot.

7 Match red dots on back and sides. Beginning at tail edge, Whipstitch back to sides, stopping at end of sail blue Whipstitching.

8 Matching red hearts, Whipstitch breast portion of body gusset to sides with eggshell. Leave remaining lower portion of body open at this time to attach head.

9 With sail blue, Whipstitch head to body. Matching hearts and using eggshell, Whipstitch remaining portion of head gusset to sides and body gusset.

10 With sail blue, Whipstitch remaining edges of body gusset to sides.

Hat & Scarf

Stitching & Assembly

1 With lavender, Whipstitch hat crown pieces together to form

Advanced
Skill Level

Tuck a small gift inside this delightfully unique gift box!

Materials

- ☐ 1 sheet 7-count regular plastic canvas
- ☐ ½ artist-size sheet Darice Ultra Stiff 7-count plastic canvas
- ☐ Uniek Needloft plastic canvas yarn as listed in color key
- ☐ DMC #3 pearl cotton as listed in color key
- ☐ DMC 6-strand embroidery floss: 1 yard light shell pink #223 and as listed in color key
- ☐ #16 tapestry needle
- ☐ 1½" white pompom (optional)
- ☐ Carpet thread
- ☐ Hot-glue gun

top of hat, then Chain-Stitch crown sections following graph and Fig. 1.

Fig. 1
Chain Stitch

2 Overcast top edge of hat cuff with lavender, overlapping three holes before Overcasting. Chain-Stitch following graph and Fig. 1.

3 Slip hat band over bottom of hat crown. Whipstitch bottom edges together with lavender.

4 If using pre-made 1½" pompom, glue to top center of hat. If making pompom, wrap 3 yards white yarn around fingers; tie tightly with a length of white yarn at center. Clip open loops and fray yarn. Glue or sew to top center of hat.

5 Chain-Stitch scarf and scarf ends following graphs and Fig. 1. With lavender, Overcast end of scarf where indicated.

6 For scarf fringe, following Fig. 2, cut 10 (4"–5") lengths of Christmas green yarn and attach to scarf ends with a Lark's Head Knot where indicated on graphs. Trim evenly.

Fig. 2
Lark's Head Knot

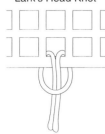

7 Using photo as a guide, with light shell pink floss, attach scarf ends to unstitched end of scarf. Wrap scarf around bird's neck, overlapping ends and placing Overcast end of scarf on top. Tack together with light shell pink floss.

8 Glue hat to top of head.

Box

Stitching & Assembly

1 Using white through step 8, Continental Stitch post top. Stitch angle pieces, post sides and box sides following graphs.

2 For each lid side, center and overlap one hole of one lid lip behind lid side, then stitch lid side as graphed. *Note: Bottom portion of lid lips will remain unstitched.*

3 Whipstitch diagonal sides of four uppermost angles together; Set aside remaining four uppermost angles.

4 Whipstitch top edges of assembled uppermost angle sides to post top. Whipstitch post sides together, then Whipstitch top edges of post sides to bottom edges of assembled uppermost angles.

5 With carpet thread, securely sew bird to post top at heels and ends of outer toes.

6 Whipstitch top edge of one center angle to 11-hole edge of one remaining uppermost angle. Repeat with remaining angle pieces. Whip-stitch diagonal sides

Snowbirdie Box

of uppermost angles together, then Whipstitch diagonal sides of center angles together.

7 Whipstitch bottom edges of post sides to uppermost angles. Whipstitch lid sides together. Whipstitch top edges of lids sides to bottom edges of center angles to complete lid.

8 Whipstitch box sides together, then Whipstitch box sides to unstitched box bottom. Overcast top edges of box sides. ●

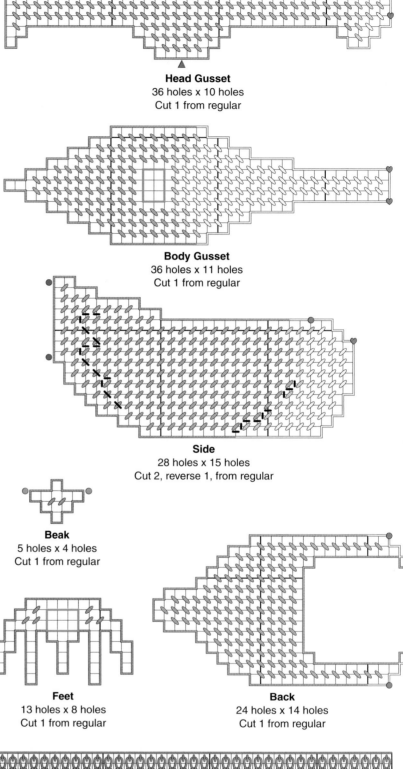

Head Gusset
36 holes x 10 holes
Cut 1 from regular

Body Gusset
36 holes x 11 holes
Cut 1 from regular

Side
28 holes x 15 holes
Cut 2, reverse 1, from regular

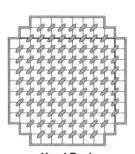

Head Back
11 holes x 12 holes
Cut 1 from regular

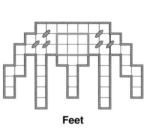

Beak
5 holes x 4 holes
Cut 1 from regular

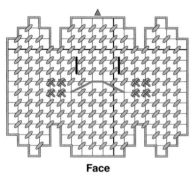

Face
17 holes x 13 holes
Cut 1 from regular

Feet
13 holes x 8 holes
Cut 1 from regular

Back
24 holes x 14 holes
Cut 1 from regular

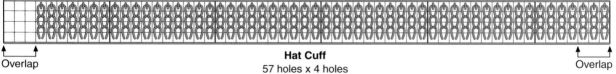

Overlap

Hat Cuff
57 holes x 4 holes
Cut 1 from regular

Overlap

Snowbirdie Box

Hat Crown
7 holes x 11 holes
Cut 6 from regular

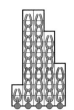

Scarf Short End
5 holes x 9 holes
Cut 1 from regular

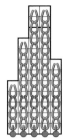

Scarf Long End
5 holes x 12 holes
Cut 1 from regular

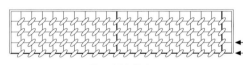

Scarf
45 holes x 2 holes
Cut 1 from regular

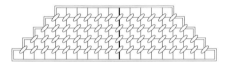

Post Uppermost Angle
19 holes x 5 holes
Cut 8 from stiff

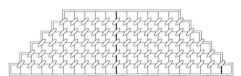

Post Center Angle
21 holes x 6 holes
Cut 4 from stiff

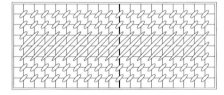

Post Side
19 holes x 8 holes
Cut 4 from stiff

Box Lid Side
21 holes x 4 holes
Cut 4 from stiff

→ Overlap with lid lip

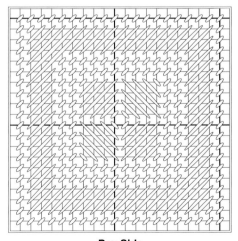

Box Side
21 holes x 21 holes
Cut 4 from stiff

COLOR KEY

Plastic Canvas Yarn	Yards
☐ Baby pink #08	2
▨ Sail blue #35	36
☐ Eggshell #39	5
▨ Beige #40	3
☐ White #41	131
⦷ Lavender #05 Chain Stitch	25
⦷ Christmas green #28 Chain Stitch	4
#3 Pearl Cotton	
✐ Black #310 Backstitch and Straight Stitch	1
6-Strand Embroidery Floss	
✖ Rose #335 Cross Stitch	1
✐ Attach legs	
✐ Attach beak	
● Attach scarf fringe	

Color numbers given are for Uniek Needloft plastic canvas yarn and DMC #3 pearl cotton and 6-strand embroidery floss.

Dickens Classic Gift Box

Design by Celia Lange Designs

A gift to share year after year

Cutting & Stitching

1 Cut outer spine from regular plastic canvas; cut front cover, pages long sides, pages short sides and hinge support from stiff plastic canvas according to graphs (pages 137 and 138).

2 Cut one 57-hole x 17-hole piece for inner spine from regular plastic canvas; cut one 47-hole x 59-hole piece for back cover and one 3-hole x 59-hole piece for hinge from stiff plastic canvas.

3 Stitch pieces following graphs, working uncoded areas, back cover, hinge and inner spine with burgundy Continental Stitches.

4 Work gold heavy (#32) braid Backstitches and Straight Stitches on front cover and outer spine when background stitching is completed.

5 Using pages long and short sides as templates, cut felt ⅛"–¼" smaller around. Glue to wrong sides, leaving room for Whipstitching and Overcasting. Cut two 6⅛" x 8⅛" pieces of cream felt. Set aside for lining lid and box bottom.

Assembly

1 Using Aran through step 2, Whipstitch short edges of pages sides together, forming box sides.

2 Whipstitch hinge support to top edges of one pages long side and around corners of pages short sides. This long side will be part of the book spine. Overcast all remaining edges.

3 Using burgundy through step 4, Overcast short edges of inner and outer spines. With right sides of all pieces facing out, Whipstitch bottom edges of inner and outer spines and one long edge of back cover together through all three thicknesses.

4 Whipstitch remaining long edges of inner and outer spines and one long edge of hinge together through all three thicknesses. **Note:** *Outer spine will bow outward.*

5 Whipstitch remaining long edge of hinge to left edge of front cover. Overcast all remaining edges.

6 Place box inside the assembled cover, aligning spine side of box with inner spine of book and placing edge of hinge over hinge support.

7 Glue spine side of box to inner spine, closing book before glue sets. Glue felt to cover back inside the box, then glue bottom edges of box sides to cover back.

8 Glue wrong side of hinge to hinge support. Glue felt lining to wrong side of front cover.

9 Using wire cutters, snap shanks off buttons; glue to front cover where indicated on graph. ●

Intermediate
Skill Level

As decorative as it is practical, this gift box looks like a favorite Christmas tale.

Materials

- ☐ 3 sheets Darice Ultra Stiff 7-count plastic canvas
- ☐ 1 sheet regular 7-count plastic canvas
- ☐ Coats & Clark Red Heart Super Saver worsted weight yarn Art. E301 as listed in color key
- ☐ Kreinik Heavy (#32) Braid as listed in color key
- ☐ #16 tapestry needle
- ☐ 2 hand-painted miniature holly buttons #92792 from JHB International Inc.
- ☐ 2 sheets cream felt
- ☐ Wire cutters
- ☐ Hot-glue gun

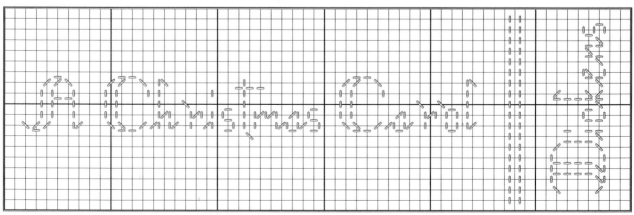

Outer Spine
59 holes x 19 holes
Cut 1 from regular

Christmas Wrappings

Dickens Classic Gift Box

COLOR KEY

Worsted Weight Yarn	Yards
☐ Aran #313	53
Uncoded areas are burgundy #376 Continental Stitches	117
◢ Burgundy #376 Overcasting and Whipstitching	
Heavy (#32) Braid	
◢ Gold #002 Backstitch and Straight Stitch	15
● Attach button	

Color numbers given are for Red Heart Super Saver worsted weight yarn Art. E301 and Kreinik Heavy (#32) Braid.

Continue pattern

Pages Long Side
55 holes x 16 holes
Cut 2 from stiff

Pages Short Side
42 holes x 16 holes
Cut 2 from stiff

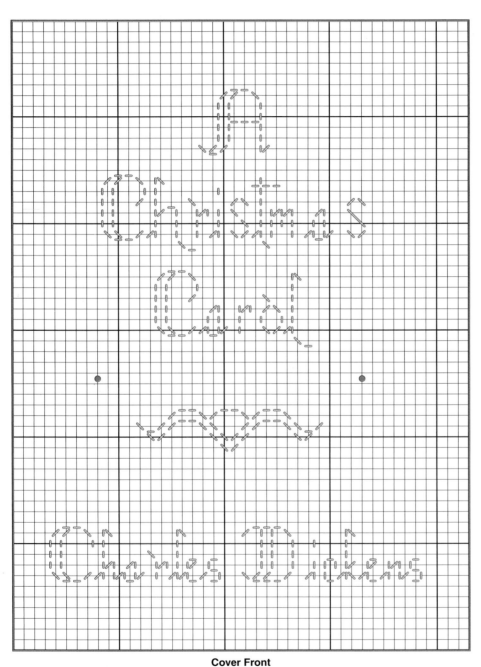

Cover Front
43 holes x 59 holes
Cut 1 from stiff

Hinge Support
2 holes x 55 holes
Cut 1 from stiff

Jolly Santa Tote

Design by Celia Lange Designs

Wish happy ho-ho-ho days with this bag

Instructions

1 Cut plastic canvas according to graphs (pages 140 and 141).

2 Stitch pieces following graphs, working nose and uncoded area on tote front with buff Continental Stitches. Stitch tote back completely with cherry red Slanting Gobelin Stitches. Reverse one eyebrow before stitching.

3 Overcast beard, mustache, eyebrows, nose and hat cuff with adjacent colors. Overcast inside edges on tote sides with cherry red.

4 Whipstitch tote front and back to tote sides with adjacent colors. With cherry red, Whipstitch tote bottom to front, back and sides; Overcast top edges.

5 Using photo as a guide through step 6, center and glue beard to tote front, making sure bottom edges are even. Glue mustache, nose, eyebrows and hat cuff in place.

6 With wire cutters, cut off side pieces of eyeglasses leaving approximately 1" length on each side.

7 Center eyeglasses over eyes and nose, then carefully insert side pieces to inside of tote. With needle-nose pliers, fold side pieces over, curling ends toward front and under slightly to prevent ends from catching on contents of tote.

8 For handle, thread ends of cord through holes on sides to inside of tote. Knot cord at desired length; trim ends as necessary. ●

Celebrate the season with this jolly Santa gift tote!

Materials

- ☐ 3 sheets Darice Ultra Stiff 7-count plastic canvas
- ☐ Coats & Clark Red Heart Super Saver worsted weight yarn Art. E301 as listed in color key
- ☐ Coats & Clark Red Heart Jeweltones worsted weight yarn Art. E278 as listed in color key
- ☐ #16 tapestry needle
- ☐ 18" 5mm red satin cord
- ☐ 3¼" oval eyeglasses
- ☐ Wire cutters
- ☐ Needle-nose pliers
- ☐ Hot-glue gun

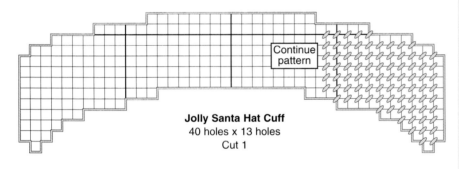

Continue pattern

Jolly Santa Hat Cuff
40 holes x 13 holes
Cut 1

Jolly Santa Mustache
22 holes x 6 holes
Cut 1

Jolly Santa Eyebrow
10 holes x 6 holes
Cut 2, reverse 1

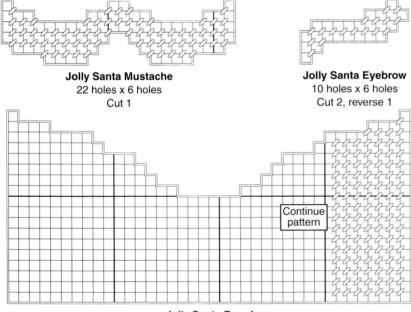

Continue pattern

Jolly Santa Beard
38 holes x 18 holes
Cut 1

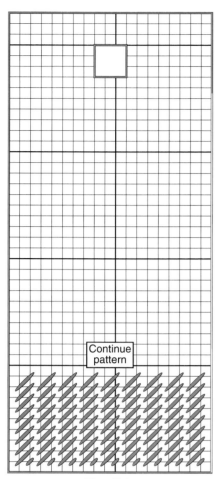

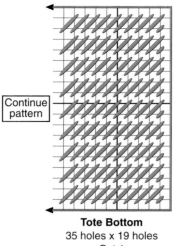

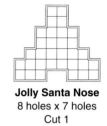

Continue pattern

Tote Bottom
35 holes x 19 holes
Cut 1

Jolly Santa Nose
8 holes x 7 holes
Cut 1

Continue pattern

Tote Side
19 holes x 43 holes
Cut 2

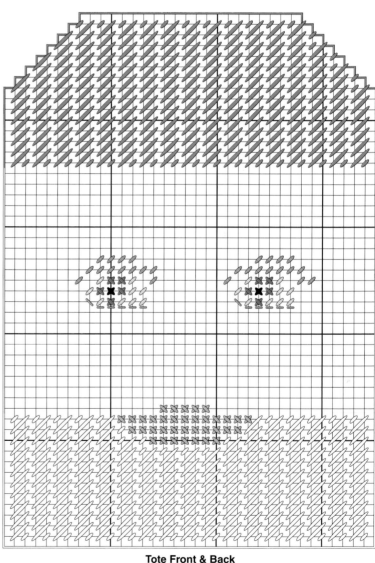

COLOR KEY

Worsted Weight Yarn	Yards
■ Black #312	1
☐ Soft White #316	18
■ Cherry red #319	61
▨ Warm brown #336	1
▨ Light coral rose #349	1
■ Windsor blue #380	1
▨ White #3311	8
Uncoded areas are buff	
#334 Continental Stitches	15

⁄ Buff #334 Overcasting and Whipstitching
⁄ Warm brown #336 Backstitch

Color numbers given are for Red Heart Super Saver worsted weight yarn Art. E301 and Red Heart Jeweltones worsted weight yarn Art. E278.

Tote Front & Back
35 holes x 50 holes
Cut 2
Stitch front as graphed
Stitch back with cherry red
Slanting Gobelin Stitches only

Happy Elves Basket

Design by Michele Wilcox

Please the young and young at heart

Instructions

1 Cut plastic canvas according to graphs (pages 142 and 143).

2 Stitch pieces following graphs, working uncoded areas on basket sides with yellow Continental Stitches.

3 Work French Knot eyes and Backstitches for mouths and between legs when background stitching is completed.

4 Overcast handle with yellow. Overcast top edges of basket with yellow and around heads with adjacent colors.

5 With sewing needle and red and green sewing thread, sew one 9mm bell to each hat where indicated on graph. Leaving 1"–1½" free on ends, evenly space 15mm bells on handle and sew in place with yellow yarn.

6 With yellow, Whipstitch basket sides together, then Whipstitch sides to bottom.

7 Glue handle ends behind hat of center elf on opposite sides of basket. ●

Beginner
Skill Level

Stitch up this basket and let Santa's happy helpers jingle their way into your heart!

Materials

- ☐ 2 sheets 7-count plastic canvas
- ☐ Uniek Needloft plastic canvas yarn as listed in color key
- ☐ DMC #5 pearl cotton as listed in color key
- ☐ #16 tapestry needle
- ☐ 12 (9mm) gold jingle bells
- ☐ 9 (15mm) gold jingle bells
- ☐ Sewing needle and red and green sewing thread to match yarn
- ☐ Hot-glue gun

Elves Basket Side
43 holes x 30 holes
Cut 4

COLOR KEY	
Plastic Canvas Yarn	**Yards**
■ Black #00	15
■ Red #01	25
■ Christmas green #28	25
☐ White #41	6
■ Flesh tone #56	12
☐ Yellow #57	60
Uncoded areas on basket sides are yellow #57 Continental Stitches	
#5 Pearl Cotton	
✎ Black #310 Backstitch	2
✎ Christmas red #321 Backstitch	2
● Black #310 French Knot	
● Attach 9mm jingle bell	
Color numbers given are for Uniek Needloft plastic canvas yarn and DMC #5 pearl cotton.	

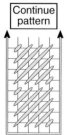

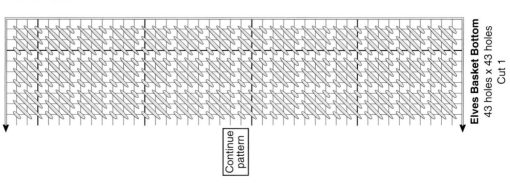

Elves Basket Handle
5 holes x 89 holes
Cut 1

Continue
pattern

Continue
pattern

Elves Basket Bottom
43 holes x 43 holes
Cut 1

Christmas Wrappings 143

Santa & Stars Basket

Design by Michele Wilcox

A perfect gift basket for Christmas Eve

Christmas Wrappings

Beginner
Skill Level

A moon-shaped Santa and golden stars adorn this keepsake holiday basket.

Materials

- 1½ sheets 7-count plastic canvas
- 4 (5") plastic canvas stars by Uniek
- Uniek Needloft plastic canvas yarn as listed in color key
- DMC #5 pearl cotton as listed in color key
- #16 tapestry needle
- Hot-glue gun

Instructions

1 Cut plastic canvas according to graphs (pages 145 and 146), cutting away gray area on stars.

2 Stitch pieces following graphs. Overcast stars, hat cuff, Santa, basket handle and top edges of basket front, back and sides with adjacent colors.

3 Work French Knot and Backstitches on Santa when background stitching and Overcasting are completed.

4 With dark royal, Whipstitch sides together, then Whipstitch sides to bottom.

5 Center and glue ends of handle inside basket front and back. Using photo as a guide, Glue Santa and stars to basket front. Glue hat cuff to Santa. ●

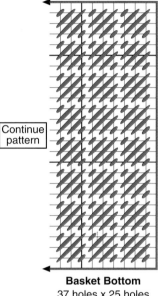

Basket Bottom
37 holes x 25 holes
Cut 1

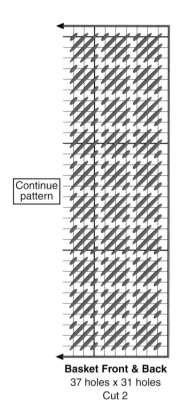

Basket Front & Back
37 holes x 31 holes
Cut 2

Basket Side
25 holes x 31 holes
Cut 2

Continue pattern

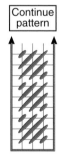

Basket Handle
4 holes x 70 holes
Cut 1

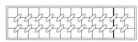

Hat Cuff
12 holes x 3 holes
Cut 1

COLOR KEY

Worsted Weight Yarn	Yards
■ Christmas red #02	3
□ Straw #19	4
□ White #41	6
■ Dark royal #48	92
▨ Flesh tone #56	1
∕ Straw #19 Backstitch	
#5 Pearl Cotton	1
∕ Black #310 Backstitch	
● Black #310 French Knot	

Color numbers given are for Uniek Needloft plastic canvas yarn and DMC #5 pearl cotton.

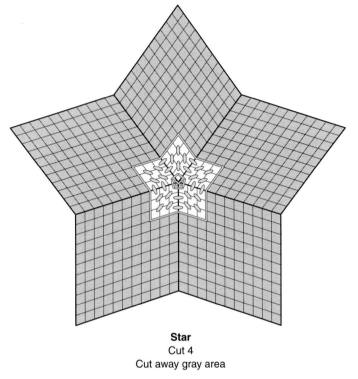

Star
Cut 4
Cut away gray area

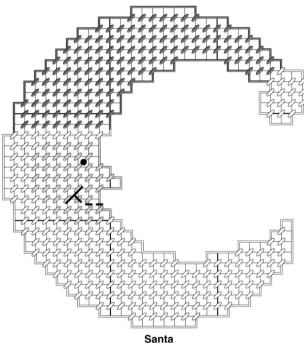

Santa
29 holes x 30 holes
Cut 1

COLOR KEY	
Worsted Weight Yarn	**Yards**
■ Christmas red #02	3
□ Straw #19	4
□ White #41	6
■ Dark royal #48	92
▨ Flesh tone #56	1
⁄ Straw #19 Backstitch	
#5 Pearl Cotton	1
✦ Black #310 Backstitch	
● Black #310 French Knot	
Color numbers given are for Uniek Needloft plastic canvas yarn and DMC #5 pearl cotton.	

Gingerbread Cutout Cookies

By Shelly Vaughan

Gingerbread People Parts

Personalizing your gingerbread people is the fun part. If you are baking with children, they will love to pick and choose their own decorating items. Pour several candies, fruits, chips and nuts into small bowls. This list may inspire you.

❤ *Eyes*—raisins, dried blueberries, miniature candy-coated chocolate candies.

❤ *Noses*—cinnamon red-hot candies, miniature candy-coated chocolate candies, dried cranberries.

❤ *Buttons*—raisins, golden raisins, cinnamon-coated raisins, dried blueberries, dried cranberries, dried cherries, small jelly beans, decorating stars, miniature candy-coated chocolate candies, chocolate chips, vanilla chips, peanut-butter chips, butterscotch chips, walnut pieces, pecan pieces, macadamia nut pieces.

❤ *Mouths*—licorice strings, almond slivers, red or pink decorating icing.

Home for Christmas

As you bring treasured friends and family into your home during the Christmas season, treat them to a delightfully decorated holiday home!

Better Not Pout!

Design by Joan Green

Look who's coming to town

Instructions

1 Cut plastic canvas according to graphs (pages 148, 150 and 171).

2 Stitch pieces following graphs, working uncoded area on sign with winter white Continental Stitches. Reverse one eyebrow before stitching. *Note: Nose and mustache area on Santa will remain unstitched.*

3 Work Backstitches and French Knots when background stitching is completed.

4 Overcast sign and hat with wine, nose with light peach, leaves with dark lagoon and all remaining edges with winter white.

5 Referring to photo for placement and using adjacent colors, attach mustache, eyebrows and pompom by tacking to Santa, working over Overcast edges in a few places to secure.

6 With wine or scarlet yarn, sew button to hat cuff where indicated on graph.

7 With white craft glue, glue small wads of bumpy doll hair on top of pompom, eyebrows and mustache.

8 Wrap chenille stems around pencil to coil. Using photo as a guide, glue one end of each stem behind beard. Glue remaining ends to top backside of sign.

9 Adjust coils as needed so sign hangs straight. Glue sawtooth hanger to top backside of hat. ●

Intermediate
Skill Level

Hang this cheerful Santa on your front door to welcome guests and put them in a happy holiday mood!

Materials

- [ ] 1 sheet 7-count plastic canvas
- [ ] Spinrite Bernat Berella "4" worsted weight yarn as listed in color key
- [ ] Spinrite plastic canvas yarn as listed in color key
- [ ] #16 tapestry needle
- [ ] White Bumples bumpy doll hair by One & Only Creations
- [ ] ½" red button
- [ ] 2 off-white chenille stems
- [ ] Sawtooth hanger
- [ ] Pencil
- [ ] Thick white craft glue

Eyebrow
7 holes x 4 holes
Cut 2, reverse 1

Holly Leaf
6 holes x 6 holes
Cut 2

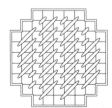

Pompom
9 holes x 9 holes
Cut 1

COLOR KEY	
Worsted Weight Yarn	**Yards**
■ Dark lagoon #8822	8
□ Rose #8921	2
■ Scarlet #8933	8
□ Winter white #8941	44
▨ Light peach #8977	6
■ Black #8994	½
Uncoded area on sign is winter white #8941 Continental Stitches	
✎ Dark lagoon #8822 Backstitch and Straight Stitch	
● Scarlet #8933 French Knot	
○ Winter white #8941 French Knot	
Plastic Canvas Yarn	
▨ Wine #0011	
Color numbers given are for Spinrite Bernat Berella "4" worsted weight yarn and Spinrite plastic canvas yarn.	

Graphs continued on page 150 and 171

Graphs continued on page 171

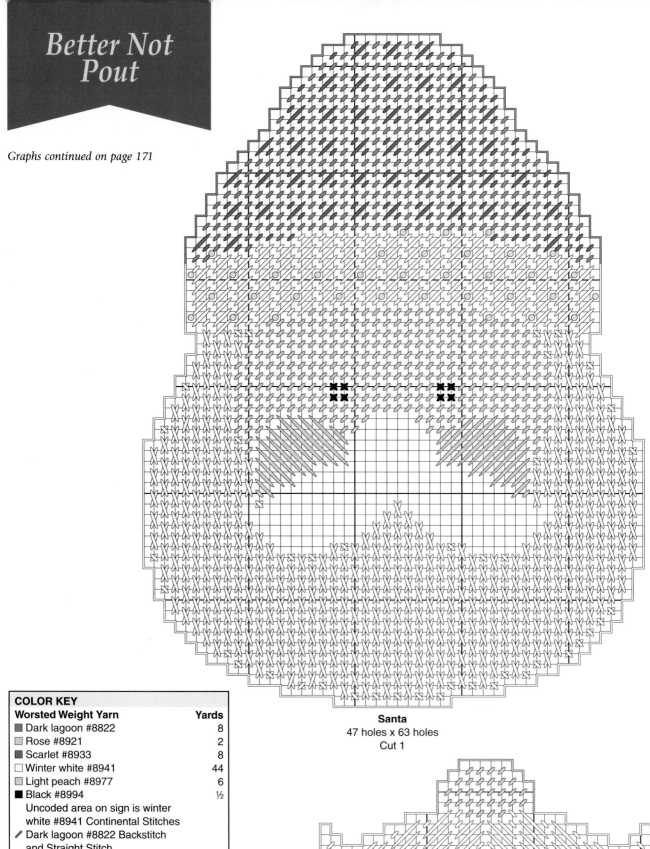

Santa
47 holes x 63 holes
Cut 1

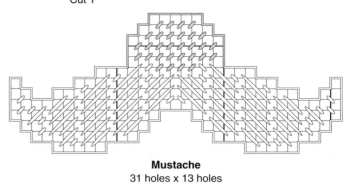

Mustache
31 holes x 13 holes
Cut 1

COLOR KEY

Worsted Weight Yarn		Yards
■	Dark lagoon #8822	8
▢	Rose #8921	2
■	Scarlet #8933	8
☐	Winter white #8941	44
▨	Light peach #8977	6
■	Black #8994	½
	Uncoded area on sign is winter white #8941 Continental Stitches	
╱	Dark lagoon #8822 Backstitch and Straight Stitch	
●	Scarlet #8933 French Knot	
○	Winter white #8941 French Knot	

Plastic Canvas Yarn

▨	Wine #0011	

Color numbers given are for Spinrite Bernat Berella "4" worsted weight yarn and Spinrite plastic canvas yarn.

Rocking Rudy

Design by Kristine Loffredo

It's time to play a reindeer game

Cutting & Stitching

1 Cut plastic canvas according to graphs (pages 152 and 153). Base bottom will remain unstitched.

2 Stitch pieces following graphs, reversing one reindeer and one ear and working pieces in Reverse Continental and Reverse Slanting Gobelin Stitches.

3 Work Backstitches on green blanket with red. Work black Straight Stitches for mouth, but do not work stitch over edge at this time.

4 Overcast short edges of base top and bottom with royal. Overcast antlers with dark brown. Using tan, Overcast ears, legs and bottom of each reindeer body; tack one ear to each head where indicated on graphs.

Assembly

1 Place wrong sides of reindeer together; with tan, Whipstitch edges together at front of face from just beneath the nose to top of neck.

2 Open reindeer slightly and work remaining black stitch for mouth from one side of face over edge to other side. Pull stitch to remove any slack, securing ends on inside.

3 Following graphs, Whipstitch reindeer edges together around nose and top of head to antlers, down front of neck to bottom of breast just above front legs, and from back of head at antlers to just above hind legs.

4 Using royal through step 5, Whipstitch long edges of base top to center top of rockers between arrows. Whipstitch long edges of base bottom to center bottom of rockers between arrows.

5 Whipstitch side edges of rockers together where indicated from blue dot to blue dot. Overcast all remaining edges of rockers.

6 Secure ears with a dot of glue placed under ear at attachment. Using photo as a guide through step 7, glue eyes where indicated on graph. Evenly space and glue three jingle bells to each side of collar. Glue holly and leaves at collar and blanket.

7 Glue one silver snowflake to center of each rocker, then glue red snowflakes to ends of rockers. Glue one jingle bell to center of each snowflake. ●

Intermediate
Skill Level

This delightful Rudolph will lead the way to your holiday fun and festivities!

Materials

- ☐ 2 sheets 7-count plastic canvas
- ☐ Worsted weight yarn as listed in color key
- ☐ #16 tapestry needle
- ☐ 2 (15mm) oval movable eyes
- ☐ 4 (1") red foil snowflakes
- ☐ 2 (1") silver foil snowflakes
- ☐ 12 (6mm) gold jingle bells
- ☐ Miniature holly leaves and berries
- ☐ Hot-glue gun

Rocker Base Top & Bottom
23 holes x 14 holes
Cut 2, stitch 1

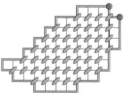

Rocking Rudy Ear
11 holes x 8 holes
Cut 2
Stitch 1 as graphed
Reverse 1 and stitch with
Reverse Continental Stitches

COLOR KEY

Worsted Weight Yarn	Yards
☐ Tan	20
■ Royal	14
■ Green	5
☐ White	4
■ Dark brown	4
■ Red	4
■ Black	2

Uncoded areas are on reindeer are tan Continental Stitches
⁄ Red Backstitch
⁄ Black Straight Stitch
● Attach ear
● Attach eye

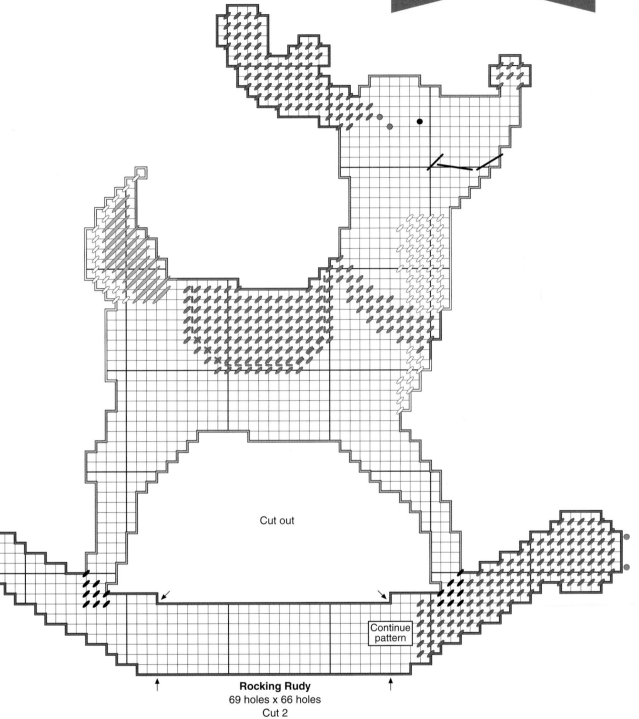

Cut out

Continue pattern

Rocking Rudy
69 holes x 66 holes
Cut 2
Stitch 1 as graphed
Reverse 1 and stitch with
Reverse Continental Stitches and
Reverse Slanting Gobelin Stitches

Holiday Lighthouse

Design by Celia Lange Designs

A project inspired by the rocky coast

Cutting & Painting

1 Cut lighthouse, base, vestibule and house pieces from stiff plastic canvas according to graphs (pages 156 and 157). Cut one 58-hole x 4-hole piece from black plastic canvas for lighthouse rail. Rail will remain unstitched.

2 For observation deck, cut the five innermost rows of holes from the plastic canvas radial circle, leaving the four outermost rows of holes.

3 Paint wooden candle cup with Santa red acrylic paint. Allow to dry.

Stitching

1 Stitch cherry red Long Stitches around circle of observation deck from the innermost row of holes to the outermost row of holes. Overcast inside edge with cherry red.

2 With black, Whipstitch short ends of rail together, then Whipstitch rail to outer edge of observation deck.

3 Stitch remaining pieces following graphs. Overcast bottom edge of vestibule front following graph. Work Backstitches on vestibule front and sides and on house sides with black pearl cotton.

4 Using adjacent colors through step 6, Overcast base. Whipstitch lighthouse sides to lighthouse corners. Overcast top and bottom edges.

5 With wrong sides together, Whipstitch top edges of corresponding vestibule and house roof pieces together. Overcast remaining roof edges.

6 Whipstitch house front and back to house sides; Overcast remaining edges. Whipstitch vestibule front to vestibule sides; Overcast remaining edges.

Assembly

1 Use photo as a guide throughout assembly. Glue painted candle cup inside top of lighthouse, then glue top edge of candle cup to center hole of observation deck.

2 Making sure bottom edges are even, center and glue vestibule to front of house, then center and glue house to one side of lighthouse.

3 Glue lighthouse, house and vestibule to base. Glue corresponding roofs to house and vestibule.

4 Glue trees as desired to base. Glue wreath to lighthouse above house.

5 For garland, glue miniature pine stem in four scallops around lighthouse. Cut ribbon into four equal lengths; tie each in a bow, trimming ends as desired. Glue bows to top points of garland.

6 Place glass votive and candle in observation deck. ●

Intermediate
Skill Level

Add a warm candlelight glow to your home with this handsome lighthouse decoration.

Materials

- ☐ 2 sheets Darice Ultra Stiff clear 7-count plastic canvas
- ☐ ⅛ sheet black 7-count plastic canvas
- ☐ 3" plastic canvas radial circle
- ☐ Coats & Clark Red Heart Super Saver worsted weight yarn Art. E301: 1 yard black #312 and as listed in color key
- ☐ Coats & Clark Red Heart Jeweltones nylon/acrylic worsted weight yarn Art. E278 as listed in color key
- ☐ DMC #3 pearl cotton as listed in color key
- ☐ #16 tapestry needle
- ☐ 18" thin wired miniature pine stem
- ☐ 2½" evergreen wreath with red bow
- ☐ 24" of ¼"-wide red satin ribbon

Continued on page 156

Materials

Continued from page 154

- ☐ DecoArt Americana Santa red #DA170 acrylic paint
- ☐ Craft paintbrush
- ☐ 1⅝" wooden candle cup
- ☐ Votive candle holder with base to fit candle cup
- ☐ Yellow votive candle
- ☐ 4 assorted sizes snow-flocked miniature Christmas trees
- ☐ Low-temperature glue gun

Continue pattern

Lighthouse Corner
6 holes x 74 holes
Cut 4 from stiff

Lighthouse Side
11 holes x 74 holes
Cut 4 from stiff

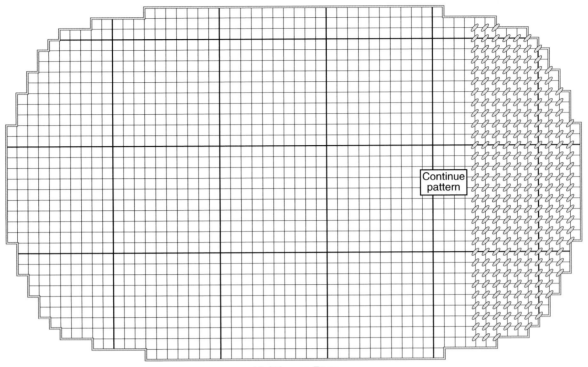

Lighthouse Base
54 holes x 33 holes
Cut 1 from stiff

Continue pattern

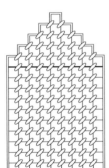

House Front & Back
9 holes x 15 holes
Cut 2 from stiff

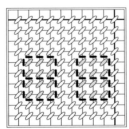

House Side
11 holes x 11 holes
Cut 2 from stiff

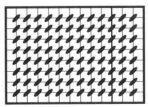

House Roof
13 holes x 9 holes
Cut 2 from stiff

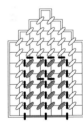

Vestibule Front
7 holes x 10 holes
Cut 1 from stiff

COLOR KEY	
Worsted Weight Yarn	**Yards**
☐ White #311	30
◼ Cherry red #319	43
☐ Bright yellow #324	2
Nylon/Acrylic Worsted Weight Yarn	
◼ Onyx #3312	9
☐ White #3311	35
#3 Pearl Cotton	
✏ Black #310 Backstitch	1

Color numbers given are for Red Heart Super Saver worsted weight yarn Art. E301 and Red Heart Jeweltones nylon/acrylic worsted weight yarn Art. E278 and DMC #3 pearl cotton.

Vestibule Roof
7 holes x 7 holes
Cut 2 from stiff

Vestibule Side
5 holes x 7 holes
Cut 2 from stiff

Poinsettia Table Accents

Designs by Mary T. Cosgrove

Quick and easy table dress-ups

Home for Christmas

Intermediate
Skill Level

Bring a bright, festive touch to your Christmas dinner table with a matching poinsettia coaster and napkin ring pair for each guest.

Materials

- ☐ 2 (5") plastic canvas stars by Uniek
- ☐ Small amount 7-count plastic canvas
- ☐ Uniek Needloft plastic canvas yarn as listed in color key
- ☐ #16 tapestry needle
- ☐ Small amount DMC dark lemon #444 6-strand embroidery floss
- ☐ 20 Whimsy yellow glass seed beads #5112 from Wichelt Imports
- ☐ Beading needle
- ☐ Hot-glue gun

Instructions

1 Cut napkin ring poinsettia from star shape and ring from plastic canvas according to graphs, cutting away gray area on star. Do not cut remaining star, which is for coaster.

2 Stitch coaster following graph. Overcast with red.

3 Overlap 4 holes on napkin ring where indicated and stitch as graphed. Overcast with eggshell.

4 Stitch petals on napkin ring poinsettia, Overcasting edges while stitching. Overcast edges of center with holly.

5 Using beading needle and 1 strand dark lemon embroidery floss, add two beads to each of the five center holes in both the napkin ring poinsettia and the coaster.

6 Attach poinsettia to overlap on ring with holly yarn by stitching over edge of each center hole, then stitching over each intersection between petal and center of flower. ●

Continue pattern around star

Coaster
Stitch 1

COLOR KEY	
Plastic Canvas Yarn	**Yards**
■ Red #01	9
■ Holly #27	4
☐ Eggshell #39	9
Color numbers given are for Uniek Needloft plastic canvas yarn.	

Napkin Ring Poinsettia
Cut 1
Cut away gray area

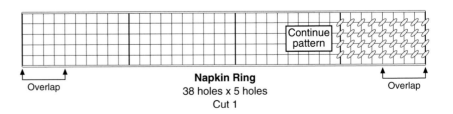

Continue pattern

Napkin Ring
38 holes x 5 holes
Cut 1

Overlap   Overlap

Christmas Mantel Decoration

Design by Celia Lange Designs

Add this accent to your home sweet home

Home for Christmas

Intermediate
Skill Level

Dress up your fireplace mantel or a shelf with this charming home accent piece.

Materials

- ☐ 2 sheets Darice Ultra Stiff clear 7-count plastic canvas
- ☐ Small amount Darice Super Soft clear 7-count plastic canvas
- ☐ Small amount brown 7-count plastic canvas
- ☐ Coats & Clark Red Heart Classic worsted weight yarn Art. E267 as listed in color key
- ☐ Coats & Clark Red Heart Jeweltones worsted weight yarn Art. E278 as listed in color key
- ☐ Darice Bright Pearls pearlized metallic cord as listed in color key
- ☐ DMC #3 pearl cotton as listed in color key
- ☐ #16 tapestry needle
- ☐ 4" frosted sisal tree
- ☐ 3" frosted sisal tree
- ☐ 1" frosted sisal wreath with red bow
- ☐ 1¾" miniature sled
- ☐ Floral clay wrapped in plastic or other weight
- ☐ Low-temperature glue gun

Cutting & Stitching

1 Cut igloo entrance sides and roof from soft plastic canvas; cut snowshoes from brown plastic canvas according to graphs (pages 163 and 164). Snowshoes will remain unstitched.

2 Cut one 89-hole x 10-hole piece from stiff plastic canvas for snow base. Cut remaining pieces as shown from stiff plastic canvas according to graphs (pages 162, 163 and 164).

3 Continental-Stitch snow base with white yarn. Continental Stitch and Overcast snowman coat and arms following graphs, reversing one arm before stitching. Work tan French Knots when stitching and Overcasting are completed.

4 Stitch remaining pieces following graphs, working uncoded background on icicles with white pearlized metallic cord Continental-Stitches.

5 When background stitching is completed, work facial features on snowman with black pearl cotton and words on icicles with dark delft pearl cotton.

6 Overcast igloo with white yarn, snowman with white and forest green yarn, snowshoes with mid brown and bottom edge of igloo entrance back with black.

Assembly

1 With white yarn, Whipstitch one long edge of snow base to bottom edge of background. Overcast sky edges with skipper blue and remaining edges of background and side edges of snow base with white yarn.

2 Using white pearlized metallic cord, Overcast side and bottom edges of icicles, then Whipstitch top edge of icicles to remaining long edge of snow base.

3 Use white through step 4. For support box, Whipstitch long sides to short sides, then Whipstitch sides to bottom. Insert plastic-wrapped floral clay or other weight in box, then Whipstitch top to sides.

4 For igloo entrance, Whipstitch one long edge of sides and roof around the side and top edges of front, then Whipstitch remaining long side of sides and roof around the side and top edges of back. Overcast remaining edges.

5 Glue support box to center back of background, making sure bottom edges are even.

6 Using photo as a guide through step 7, glue igloo and snowman to snow base and background. Glue arms to snowman and background; glue coat to snowman and arms.

7 Glue igloo entrance to base and front of igloo; center and glue wreath to entrance front. Glue on trees, snowshoes and sled.

8 Place on mantel or shelf, allowing icicles to hang over edge. ●

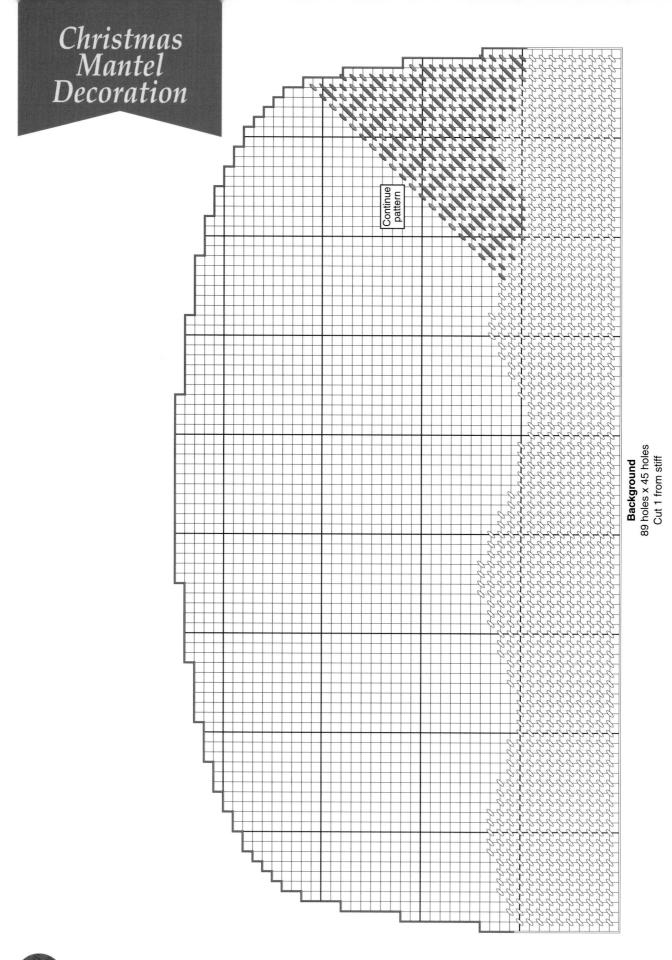

Continue pattern

Background
89 holes x 45 holes
Cut 1 from stiff

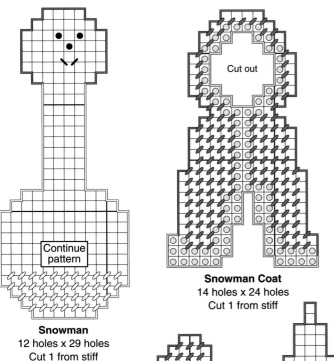

Cut out

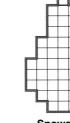

Snowman Coat
14 holes x 24 holes
Cut 1 from stiff

Continue pattern

Snowman
12 holes x 29 holes
Cut 1 from stiff

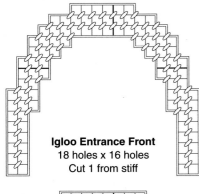

Snowman Arm
12 holes x 9 holes
Cut 2, reverse 1, from stiff

Snowshoe
7 holes x 12 holes
Cut 2 from brown
Do not stitch

COLOR KEY

Worsted Weight Yarn	Yards
■ Black #12	5
■ Forest green #689	5
■ New berry #760	1
■ Skipper blue #848	27
□ Olympic blue #849	12
□ White #3311	120
⁄ Tan #334 Overcasting	5
⁄ Mid brown #339 Overcasting	1
○ Tan #334 French Knot	
Pearlized Metallic Cord	
Uncoded background on icicles is White #3410-01 Continental Stitches	20
⁄ White #3410-01 Overcasting	
#3 Pearl Cotton	
⁄ Black #310 Backstitch	1
⁄ Dark delft #798 Backstitch and Straight Stitch	4
● Black #310 French Knot	
○ Dark delft #798 French Knot	

Color numbers given are for Red Heart Classic worsted weight yarn Art. E267 and Red Heart Jeweltones worsted weight yarn Art. E278, Darice Bright Pearls pearlized metallic cord and DMC #3 pearl cotton.

Igloo Entrance Front
18 holes x 16 holes
Cut 1 from stiff

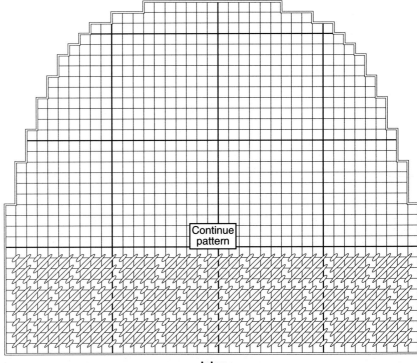

Continue pattern

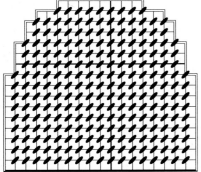

Igloo Entrance Back
18 holes x 16 holes
Cut 1 from stiff

Igloo
39 holes x 33 holes
Cut 1 from stiff

Continue pattern

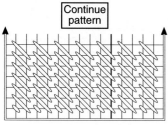

Support Box Top & Bottom
44 holes x 15 holes
Cut 2 from stiff

Continue pattern

Support Box Short Side
15 holes x 29 holes
Cut 2 from stiff

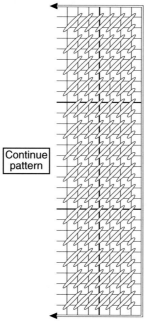

Continue pattern

Support Box Long Side
44 holes x 29 holes
Cut 2 from stiff

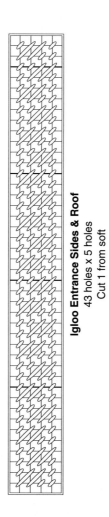

Igloo Entrance Sides & Roof
43 holes x 5 holes
Cut 1 from soft

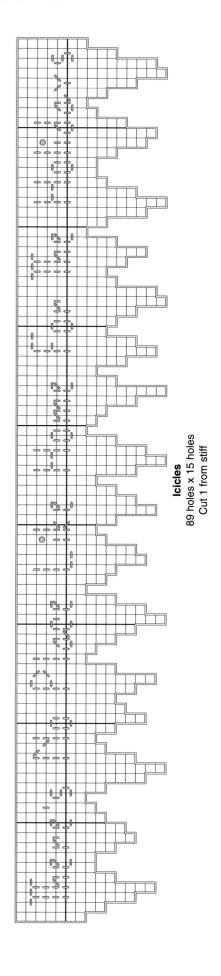

Icicles
89 holes x 15 holes
Cut 1 from stiff

COLOR KEY	
Worsted Weight Yarn	**Yards**
■ Black #12	5
■ Forest green #689	5
■ New berry #760	1
■ Skipper blue #848	27
□ Olympic blue #849	12
□ White #3311	120
✎ Tan #334 Overcasting	5
✎ Mid brown #339 Overcasting	1
○ Tan #334 French Knot	
Pearlized Metallic Cord	
Uncoded background on icicles is White #3410-01 Continental Stitches	20
✎ White #3410-01 Overcasting	
#3 Pearl Cotton	
✐ Black #310 Backstitch	1
✎ Dark delft #798 Backstitch and Straight Stitch	4
● Black #310 French Knot	
○ Dark delft #798 French Knot	

Color numbers given are for Red Heart Classic worsted weight yarn Art. E267 and Red Heart Jeweltones worsted weight yarn Art. E278, Darice Bright Pearls pearlized metallic cord and DMC #3 pearl cotton.

"I Believe" Wall Hanging

Design by Michele Wilcox

Santa is waving through the window!

Stitch this festive wall hanging to add to the Christmas cheer throughout the season!

Instructions

1 Cut plastic canvas according to graphs (pages 166 and 167).

2 Stitch frame following graph, leaving center area unstitched. Overcast with red.

3 Stitch front piece following graph, working uncoded areas inside the window with dark royal Continental Stitches and uncoded areas outside the window with white Continental Stitches. Overcast with red.

4 When background stitching is completed, work holly berry French Knots with red yarn. Work eyes, mouth and letters with pearl cotton.

5 Thread ends of wire through holes indicated on frame; pull wire through, leaving about 6" for hanger. Wrap ends around top of hanger, then curl around pencil. Remove pencil and trim to desired length.

6 Place cardboard on unstitched canvas in center of frame, trimming as necessary to fit. Center and glue front piece to frame. ●

Materials

- ☐ 2 sheets 7-count plastic canvas
- ☐ Uniek Needloft plastic canvas yarn as listed in color key
- ☐ #3 pearl cotton as listed in color key
- ☐ #16 tapestry needle
- ☐ 6¾" x 9⅜" piece cardboard
- ☐ 24" green wire
- ☐ Pencil
- ☐ Hot-glue gun

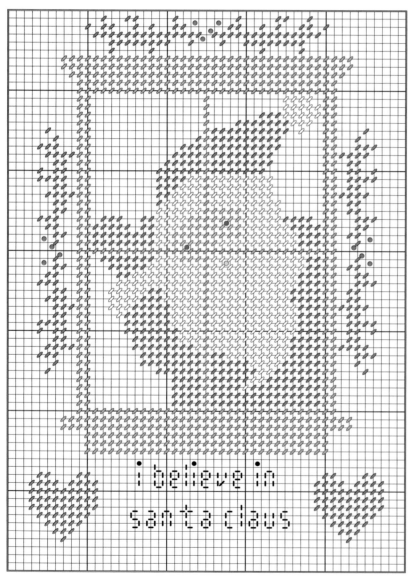

Front Piece
50 holes x 70 holes
Cut 1

COLOR KEY	
Plastic Canvas Yarn	**Yards**
■ Red #01	10
■ Christmas green #28	55
■ Cerulean #34	12
☐ White #41	30
■ Flesh tone #56	1
Uncoded areas outside the window are white #41 Continental Stitches	
Uncoded areas inside the window are dark royal #48 Continental Stitches	8
● Red #01 French Knot	
#3 Pearl Cotton	
╱ Black Backstitch	3
● Black French Knot	
○ Red French Knot	⅙
● Blue French Knot	⅙
X Attach wire	
Color numbers given are for Uniek Needloft plastic canvas yarn.	

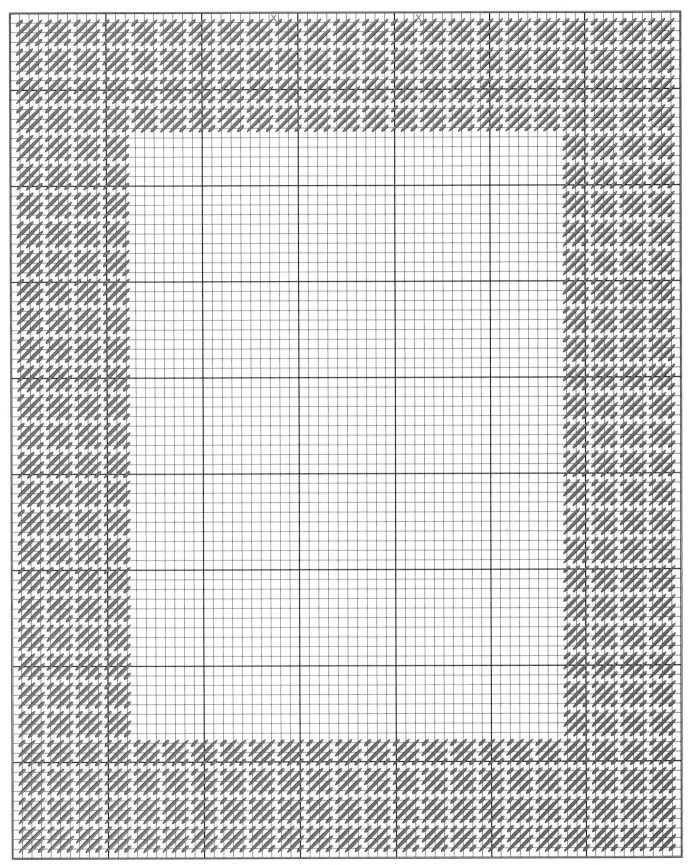

Frame
70 holes x 88 holes
Cut 1

Snowman
Door Hanger

Design by Celia Lange Designs

Let it snow inside or out

Intermediate
Skill Level

Add a festive accent to your front door during the holiday season with this friendly snowman!

Instructions

1. Cut door hanger and snowman pieces from 7-count clear plastic canvas; cut snowflakes from 10-count white plastic canvas according to graphs (pages 169 and 170), cutting away blue lines on snowflake graphs.

2. Stitch pieces following graphs. Snowflakes will remain unstitched.

3. Using black pearl cotton, add French Knot eyes and mouth; using cherry red yarn, add French Knot buttons. Straight Stitch nose using orange yarn.

4. Using adjacent colors, Overcast edges. Add fringe to top of hat with cherry yarn.

5. Using photo as a guide through step 6, glue head, body middle and body bottom together. Tie plaid ribbon scarf around neck.

6. Glue scraps of Spanish moss to door hanger. Glue snowman to door hanger, adding twig arms. Glue pinecones at bottom.

7. With sewing needle and thread, tack snowflakes to door hanger where indicated on graph. ●

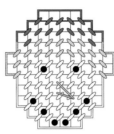

Head
10 holes x 11 holes
Cut 1 from 7-count clear

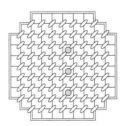

Middle Body
10 holes x 10 holes
Cut 1 from 7-count clear

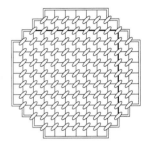

Bottom Body
12 holes x 12 holes
Cut 1 from 7-count clear

Small Snowflake
7 holes x 7 holes
Cut 2 from 10-count white, cutting away blue lines
Do not stitch

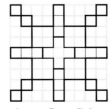

Large Snowflake
9 holes x 9 holes
Cut 3 from 10-count white, cutting away blue lines
Do not stitch

COLOR KEY	
Worsted Weight Yarn	**Yards**
☐ White #1	8
▨ Light periwinkle #347	15
▩ Hunter green #389	4
▨ Paddy green #686	4
☐ Cherry red #912	3
▨ Cardinal #917	1
╱ Orange #245 Straight Stitch	⅛
○ Cherry red #912 French Knot	
#3 Pearl Cotton	
● Black #310 French Knot	2
● Attach small snowflake	
○ Attach large snowflake	

Color numbers given are for Red Heart Classic worsted weight yarn Art. E267 and Super Saver worsted weight yarn Art. E301 and DMC #3 pearl cotton.

Snowman
Door Hanger

COLOR KEY

Worsted Weight Yarn	Yards
☐ White #1	8
☐ Light periwinkle #347	15
☐ Hunter green #389	4
☐ Paddy green #686	4
☐ Cherry red #912	3
☐ Cardinal #917	1
╱ Orange #245 Straight Stitch	⅛
○ Cherry red #912 French Knot	

#3 Pearl Cotton

● Black #310 French Knot	2
● Attach small snowflake	
○ Attach large snowflake	

Color numbers given are for Red Heart Classic
worsted weight yarn Art. E267 and Super
Saver worsted weight yarn Art. E301 and
DMC #3 pearl cotton.

Door Hanger
29 holes x 69 holes
Cut 1 from 7-count clear

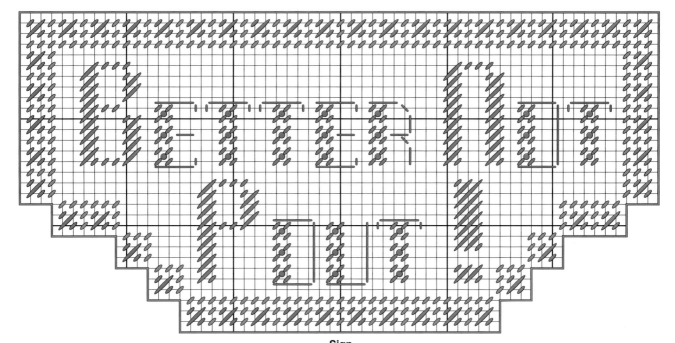

Sign
60 holes x 30 holes
Cut 1

COLOR KEY	
Worsted Weight Yarn	**Yards**
■ Dark lagoon #8822	8
□ Rose #8921	2
■ Scarlet #8933	8
□ Winter white #8941	44
□ Light peach #8977	6
■ Black #8994	½
Uncoded area on sign is winter white #8941 Continental Stitches	
╱ Dark lagoon #8822 Backstitch and Straight Stitch	
● Scarlet #8933 French Knot	
○ Winter white #8941 French Knot	
Plastic Canvas Yarn	
■ Wine #0011	
Color numbers given are for Spinrite Bernat Berella "4" worsted weight yarn and Spinrite plastic canvas yarn.	

Stitch Guide

Use the following diagrams to expand your plastic canvas stitching skills. For each diagram, bring needle up through canvas at the red number one and go back down through the canvas at the red number two. The second stitch is numbered in green. Always bring needle up through the canvas at odd numbers and take it back down through the canvas at the numbers.

Background Stitches

The following stitches are used for filling in large areas of canvas. The Continental Stitch is the most commonly used stitch. Other stitches, such as the Condensed Mosaic and Scotch Stitch, fill in large areas of canvas more quickly than the Continental Stitch because their stitches cover a larger area of canvas.

Continental Stitch

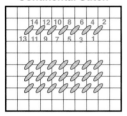

Condensed Mosaic

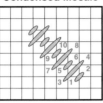

Running Stitch

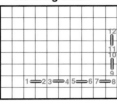

Cross Stitch

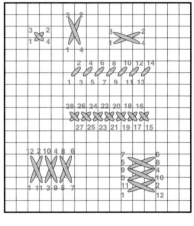

Alternating Continental

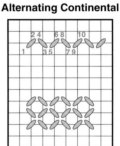
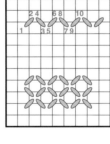

Long Stitch

Slanting Gobelin

Scotch Stitch

Embroidery Stitches

These stitches are worked on top of a stitched area to add detail to the project. Embroidery stitches are usually worked with one strand of yarn, several strands of pearl cotton or several strands of embroidery floss.

Lattice Stitch

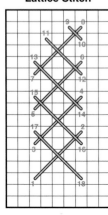

Chain Stitch

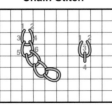

Straight Stitch

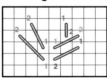

Fly Stitch

Couching

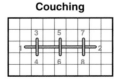

Backstitch

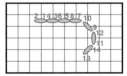

Embroidery Stitches

French Knot

Bring needle up through canvas.

Wrap yarn around needle 2 or 3 times, depending on desired size of knot; take needle back through canvase through same hole.

Lazy Daisy

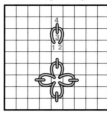

Bring yarn needle up through canvas, then back down in same hole, leaving a small loop.

Then, bring needle up inside loop; take needle back down through canvas on other side of loop.

Loop Stitch or Turkey Loop Stitch

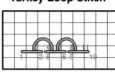

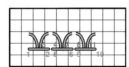

The top diagram shows this stitch left intact. This is an effective stitch for giving a project dimensional hair. The bottom diagram demonstrates the cut loop stitch. Because each stitch is anchored, cutting it will not cause the stitches to come out. A group of cut loop stitches gives a fluffy, soft look and feel to your project.

Specialty Stitches

The following stitches can be worked either on top of a previously stitched area or directly onto the canvas. Like the embroidery stitches, these too add wonderful detail and give your stitching additional interest and texture.

Diamond Eyelet

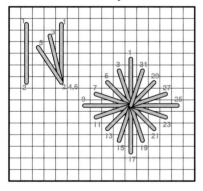

For each stitch, bring needle up at odd numbers around outside and take needle down through canvas at center hole.

Smyrna Cross

Satin Stitches

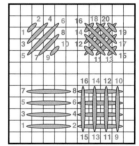

This stitch gives a "padded" look to your work.

Finishing Stitches

Overcast/Whipstitch

Overcasting and Whipstitching are used to finish the outer edges of the canvas. Overcasting is done to finish one edge at a time. Whipstitch is used to stitch two or more pieces of canvas together along on edge. For both Overcasting and Whipstitching, work one stitch in each hole along straight edges and inside corners, and two or three stitches in outside corners.

Lark's Head Knot

The Lark's Head Knot is used for a fringe edge or for attaching a hanging loop.

Buyer's Guide

Buyer's Guide

When looking for a specific material, first check your local craft and retail stores. If you are unable to locate a product locally, contact the manufacturers listed below for the closest retail source in your area or a mail-order source.

The Adhesive Products, Inc.
520 Cleveland Ave.
Albany, CA 94710
(510) 526-7616

Adhesive Technologies, Inc.
3 Merrill Industrial Dr.
Hampton, NH 03842-1995
(800) 458-3486
www.adhesivetech.com

All Cooped Up Designs
934 N. Industrial Park Dr.
Orem, UT 84057
(800) 498-1517

The Beadery Craft Products
105 Canonchet Rd.
P.O. Box 178
Hope Valley, RI 02832
(401) 539-2432

Coats & Clark
Consumer Service
P.O. Box 12229
Greenville, SC 29612-0229
(800) 648-1479
www.coatsandclark.com

Creative Beginnings
P.O. Box 1330
Morro Bay, CA 93442
(800) 367-1739

Daniel Enterprises
306 McKay St.
P.O. Box 1105
Laurinburg, NC 28353
(910) 277-7441

Darice mail order source:
Bolek's
P.O. Box 465
330 N. Tuscarawas Ave.
Dover, OH 44622
(330) 364-8878

DecoArt
P.O. Box 386
Stanford, KY 40484
(800) 367-3047

Delta Technical Coatings
2550 Pellissier Pl.
Whittier, CA 90601
(800) 423-4135

The DMC Corp.
Hackensack Ave. Bldg. 10A
South Kearny, NJ 07032
(800) 275-4117
www.dmcusa.com

Duncan Enterprises
5673 E. Shields Ave.
Fresno, CA 93727
(559) 291-4444
www.duncan-enterprises.com

Gay Bowles Sales Inc.
P.O. Box 1060
Janesville, WI 53545
(800) 447-1332
http://www.millhill.com

JHB International Inc.
1955 S. Quince St.
Denver, CO 90746
(303) 751-8100

Kreinik Mfg. Co. Inc.
3106 Timanus Ln., #101
Baltimore, MD 21244
(800) 537-2166

Lion Brand
34 W. 15th St.
New York, NY 10011
(212) 243-8995

National Artcraft Co.
7996 Darrow Rd.
Twinsburg, OH 44087
(888) 937-2723

One & Only Creations
P.O. Box 2730
Napa, CA 94558
(800) 262-6768

Rainbow Gallery mail order source:
Designs by Joan Green
1130 Tollgate Dr.
Oxford, OH 45056
(513) 523-2690

Spinrite Inc.
P.O. Box 435
Lockport, NY 14094-0435
(800) 265-2864

Box 40
Listowel, Ontario
Canada N4W 3H3
(519) 291-3780

Uniek mail order source:
Annie's Attic Catalog
1 Annie Ln.
Big Sandy, TX 75755
(800) 582-6643

Vacor USA L.L.C.
P.O. Box 21292
Wichita, KS 67208-7292
(800) 846-4228

Walnut Hollow Farm Inc.
1409 State Rd. 23
Dodgeville, WI 53533
(800) 950-5101

Westrim Crafts/Western Trimming Corp.
9667 Canoga Ave.
P.O. Box 3879
Chatsworth, CA 91313
(818) 998-8550

Wichelt Imports, Inc.
N162 Hwy. 35
Stoddard, WI 54658
(608) 788-4600

Wrights
Wm. E. Wright Ltd. Ptr.
P.O. Box 398
West Warren, MA 01092
(413) 436-7732 Ext. 445

Special Thanks

We would like to acknowledge and thank the following designers whose original work has been published in this collection. We appreciate and value their creativity and dedication to designing quality plastic canvas projects.

Angie Arickx
Keepsake Christmas Frame, Merry Christmas Blocks, Musical Ball, Peek-a-Boo Bear Stocking, Poinsettia Garland Basket, Poinsettia Gift Bag, Sparkling Snowflakes, Star of Bethlehem, Teddy in a Heart Basket, Winter Spruce Table Set

Vicki Blizzard
Christmas Tree Marble Game, Holiday Tartan Jewelry, Jingle Bell Stars, Patchwork Tree Basket, Pet Clocks, Snow Angel, Snow Crystals, Very Merry Ornaments

Mary T. Cosgrove
Baby's First Christmas, Country Home Accents, Country Pine Stocking, Little Angel Bear, Poinsettia Table Accents

Janelle Giese
From Our House to Yours, Snowbirdie Box

Joan Green
Angelic Bear, Better Not Pout!, "Peace" Santa Wreath, Teddy Bear Pocket Pals

Judi Kauffman
Poinsettia Napkin Ring

Celia Lange & Martha Bleidner of Celia Lange Designs
Christmas Mantel Decoration, Christmas Tree Gift Bag, "Dear Santa," Dickens Classic Gift Box, Gingerbread Wall Plaque, Hearts Come Home Ornament, Holiday Lighthouse, Holiday Seed Packets, Jolly Santa Tote, Mr. Snowman's Bath, Santa's Helpers, Sled Ride Centerpiece, Snowball Stand Tissue Topper, Snow Globe Coasters, Snowman Door Hanger, "Waiting for Santa" Christmas Card Box, Winter Birdhouses

Kristine Loffredo
Rocking Rudy

Alida Macor
Frame a Christmas Memory, Snowman Place Cards

Nancy Marshall
Country Rag Basket, Santa & Friends Button Covers

Kimberly A. Suber
Cheery Snowman Picture, Christmas Candle Match Holder, Festive Frames

Ruby Thacker
Teddy in a Wagon

Michele Wilcox
Beary Christmas Bag, Happy Elves Basket, "I Believe" Wall Hanging, Santa & Stars Basket, Santa Mouse Coasters, Sleepy Mouse Door Hanger